REMBRANDT

REMBRANDT

JOSEPH-EMILE MULLER

134 plates
58 in colour

LONDON
THAMES AND HUDSON

TRANSLATED FROM THE FRENCH BY
BRIAN HOOLEY

THIS EDITION © 1968 THAMES AND HUDSON, LONDON
© 1968 EDITIONS AIMERY SOMOGY S.A., PARIS
PRINTED IN GERMANY
NOT FOR SALE IN THE U.S.A.

Contents

CHAPTER ONE

Son of a miller

No one can say what makes an artist. We know that Rembrandt was born at Leyden on 15 July 1606, that he was the sixth of a family of seven children, that his father Harmen Gerritszoon worked a mill near the Rhine (whence the name van Rijn), that his mother Neeltge Willemsdochter van Zuytbroek was a baker's daughter. About the origins of Rembrandt the citizen we are well informed, yet what do these details tell us of the origins of Rembrandt the artist?

The normal career in Rembrandt's family was one of the manual professions: one of his brothers was to follow his father into milling, while another became a baker, and a third a cobbler. Who or what prompted the youngest boy to devote himself to artistic creation we do not know. Nor do we know at what point of time or in what circumstances his talent was revealed to him, nor what was the feeling of dissatisfaction with everyday life which made him want to produce a more exciting reality for which he alone would be responsible. These are questions for which no answers will ever be found.

We are told that his mother inspired him with a love of the Bible, thus providing him with one of his main sources of inspiration. But others before him had loved the Bible without dreaming of becoming artists. In the normal way such men would become priests, pastors or theologians. One may indeed wonder whether Rembrandt's parents did not have a career of this sort in mind for their son when they sent him to a school whose main emphasis was on the study of Latin. He seems to have gone to this school at the age of seven, and to have left it when he was fourteen. It is not known whether he was a keen scholar, but we may assume from the fact that he decided to continue with these studies that he cannot have found them disagreeable. During this period he learned the language of ancient Rome, which was also the language of humanism. He was also introduced to Greek and Roman literature, history, and civilization. This acquaintance helps to explain some of the subjects which he was later to use in his paintings, but was not enough to turn him into a lover of books or a philosopher.

For almost half a century before Rembrandt's birth, Leyden had been the proud possessor of the first and most famous university of the Netherlands. Subjects taught there included science as well as theology, and courses were attended by large numbers of Dutch, and even foreign, students. On 20 May 1620, Rembrandt enrolled at the university. Doubts about his choice of career, however, which he must already have experienced on previous occasions, soon crystallized into the certain knowledge that he was not cut out to be a pastor, theologian, scholar, or lawyer. The only thing which really attracted him was painting. He therefore decided to leave the university and to begin an apprenticeship with a painter. His parents' choice fell on Jacob van Swanenburgh, a local man whom they knew, and who enjoyed a reputation made all the more secure by the fact that his father was also an artist. It was generally agreed that, despite his reputation, Swanenburgh's work represented nothing out of the ordinary. But men of genius rarely make good teachers, and Rembrandt's first need was for someone who would introduce him to the rudiments of his profession. This teacher was able to do just that for his pupil. He had spent part of his life in Rome and Naples, and obviously told Rembrandt of what he had seen and admired in Italy, for Swanenburgh was one of those Northern artists who thought it impossible to produce a painting without following Italian models.

Rembrandt was to encounter another admirer of Italian art when, around 1624, he found a new master, this time not in Leyden but in

8

1 *Lastman, Pieter. The Meeting of Jacob and Laban*

Amsterdam. Pieter Lastman, who now took over as Rembrandt's instructor, had been in Rome in the early 1600s, at the time when Caravaggio was launching his artistic thunderbolts to a mixture of censure and applause. It would have been natural for Lastman to tell Rembrandt about this innovator who not only created violent tensions between light and dark in his paintings, but who also, reacting against the insipidity to which the cult of the beautiful had finally reduced certain of Raphael's successors, depicted a humanity at once simple, coarse, passionate and solemn. A painter whom Lastman seems to have held in even greater esteem than Caravaggio was Adam Elsheimer of Frankfurt. Elsheimer, with whom Lastman had maintained friend- ly relations during his stay in Rome, adopted Caravaggio's chiaroscuro, but replaced its violent aspect with more dreamy, lyrical and romantic effects.

Rembrandt no doubt listened closely to what his master had to say about the importance attached by many of Caravaggio's successors to the use of light, especially as not all such painters were Italian. In Utrecht, not far from Leyden, there was in fact a group of artists who were firm disciples of Caravaggio's principles. While still producing canvases in which figures and objects were set in ordinary daylight, Hendrick Terbrugghen, Gerard van Honthorst and others were particularly fond of using artificial lighting effects in which sharp contrasts were established between light and shade. It was not, however, these artists of Utrecht who introduced chiaroscuro to Dutch painting. Already, at the end of the fifteenth century, Gerard de Saint-Jean had painted a *Nativity* where the contrast between light and darkness was no less an important feature than the characters themselves. We cannot be sure that Rembrandt ever had the chance to see this picture, but he certainly knew, and was influenced by, the Caravaggians in Utrecht. Another influence on his painting was Lastman, who imparted to his pupil his taste for historical subjects, solemn and ordered composition, and expressive postures and gestures. Apart from this, Lastman was responsible for strengthening the interest which Rembrandt's mother had already brought to bear on biblical subjects.

After studying for six months with Lastman (and also perhaps for a short period with Jacob Pynas, another history painter and disciple of Italian art), Rembrandt went back to Leyden and before long had set up his own studio there. At about this time Rembrandt became friendly with a fellow artist, Jan Lievens. Lievens, although one year Rembrandt's junior, had finished his apprenticeship with Lastman before Rembrandt began his own with van Swanenburgh. In the course of frequent meetings the two young painters came to realize that their interests coincided, and they decided to work together in a studio which Rembrandt is believed to have set up in his parents' house. Since their subject-matter was similar and they sometimes shared the same models, the difference in their work was sometimes so slight that one wonders to which artist certain paintings ought to be attributed, while there are others to which both of them can be supposed to have lent a hand.

Despite his youth Rembrandt soon managed to attract attention. As early as 1628 Aernout van Buchell, a jurist from Utrecht who came to Leyden on a journey, observed that a miller's son was held in high repute in the town—although, he added, such praise was premature. Shortly after this Constantijn Huygens, secretary to the Prince Regent Frederick Henry of Orange, also went to Leyden, and when, between 1629 and 1631, he began to write his autobiography, he also mentioned Rembrandt and Lievens. Constantijn Huygens was no ordinary man. He had a good all-round cultural education; he was able to express himself in several languages, he wrote poetry, was something of a musician, and took an interest in science. He also maintained a correspondence with Descartes. Most important, he was a lover of art, being familiar with Flemish and Venetian painting (which he had seen in Venice itself) as well as that of his own country. His verdict was therefore less summary than van Buchell's, and carried more weight. *Ill. 3*

It is significant in itself that Huygens, in a text which stresses the merits of artists of such repute as Goltzius, Mierevelt, Porcellis, Cornelis van Haarlem, van Goyen, Esaias van de Velde and others, and proclaims his admiration for Rubens ('one of the wonders of the world'), should go out of his way to mention two young men, barely more than twenty years old, whose artistic equipment was of necessity not yet highly developed. But even more striking are the terms he uses to describe them, for he has no hesitation in declaring that the two youths of Leyden were already the equal of the most famous contemporary painters and that before long they would surpass them. Their humble origins—while Rembrandt's father was a miller, Lievens' was an embroiderer—provided, in his opinion, a complete refutation of the theory that noble blood was more resourceful than commoners'. The limited means of their parents, Huygens comments, had allowed them to study only under mediocre teachers who, had they been able to see their former pupils at that moment, 'would have been as ashamed as those who taught Virgil, Cicero, or Archimedes.' He goes so far as to say that the two young men owed nothing to their teachers, and would have reached the same standard even without instruction.

Commenting on the special characteristics of each painter, Huygens judged Rembrandt to be superior to Lievens in his discernment and in

2 Hannemann, A.
Portrait of Constantijn Huygens

3 Lievens, Jan.
Child blowing Soap Bubbles

the vividness with which he expressed emotions, while Lievens, in his opinion, held the edge in inventiveness and boldness. Huygens thought the small, carefully executed paintings of Rembrandt, however, possessed a force of expression not to be found in his colleague's work. His *Judas returning the Thirty Pieces of Silver*, for instance, compared more than favourably to 'anything produced by the ancients or by Italian artists. With this work, the callow son of a Batavian miller surpasses Protogenes, Apelles and Parrhasius.' Clearly, Huygens was here quoting names which had long stood, in contemporary eyes, for all that was best in painting. (Such opinion, incidentally, was grounded on texts rather than on a first-hand appraisal of works which had long since been lost.)

The enthusiastic commentator, convinced by this *Judas* that Rembrandt was a great painter of historical subjects, also had a criticism to make of the two young artists. They felt there was no need for them to go to Italy, but Huygens suggested that a period spent familiarizing themselves with the creations of Raphael and Michelangelo would raise them to the very peak of the artistic profession. The artists' reply to this was that such a journey could not for the moment be contemplated—they could not spare the time. In any case, it was their opinion that the best Italian paintings were to be found outside Italy, while in Italy itself they had to be hunted down in a great number of places a good distance apart. Huygens did not venture to question the validity of this reply, though he most likely had his doubts, but he affirmed that he had rarely seen such enthusiasm and endurance. Rembrandt and Lievens were more like boys than youths to look at, and denied themselves the usual pleasures of young men of their age. The Prince Regent's secretary, who appreciated the value of physical exercise, expressed the wish that they would take greater care of their bodies, for, he said, they lacked sturdiness and were not improved by the sedentary life they led.

It may well be said that the paintings over which Huygens went into raptures cannot be counted among Rembrandt's most moving works. None the less, his appreciation of the painter was not lacking in insight. What is most notable is that, right from the beginning, Rembrandt was commanding recognition; a well-informed observer like Huygens could find authority in his work and detect, in the few canvases Rembrandt had then completed, the promise of an exceptional career. The young painter himself can hardly have failed to share this opinion and, despite his youthfulness, must have felt he was already a master painter. For he had barely left Lastman's studio when he took in two pupils of his own—Gerard Dou and Jan Joris van Vliet. Dou was still only a child, but van Vliet was an etcher whom Rembrandt encouraged to make engravings based on his own paintings. In this way his art became known not only within Leyden, but spread to other towns, and in particular to Amsterdam.

CHAPTER TWO

Art in a Calvinist country

At the time when Rembrandt was establishing his reputation as a painter in Leyden, Holland found herself once more at war with Spain. The twelve-years truce agreed to in 1609 had expired a few years before. This truce had put an end to hostilities which, in their early stages, had been a severe trial for the United Provinces. Leyden in particular had fared badly, the terrible siege of 1574 costing the town one half of its population. In the end, however, the sufferings and sorrows which the revolt against Spanish tutelage involved brought the Dutch a series of dazzling successes. Holland became a sovereign republic of rapidly accumulating wealth. The powerful fleet which the war had led her to create did more than confine its activities to fighting the enemy—it also undertook the exploration and exploitation of distant lands. The Dutch East India Company, founded in 1602, sent back a stream of boats laden with fabulous produce from the Far East, while the Dutch West India Company, established in 1623, concentrated on Africa and the New World.

Even the renewal of hostilities with Spain failed to undermine the newly won independence, or the prosperity of those who had managed to enrich themselves. In any case, the main theatres of war were now the sea and the border areas. Thus it was that in 1625 the town of Breda, after heroic resistance to a siege, finally had to surrender to Spinola, an Italian general in the service of Spain. Velazquez was to commemorate the event ten years later in a painting which combined the virtues of the spirit of chivalry with those of his own admirably fluent and precise style.

There is no reason why Rembrandt should also have portrayed the surrender of Breda, but it would be interesting to know whether this national defeat affected him and whether he was in general concerned by events in the political sphere. Everything points to the conclusion that he was not interested in politics, that his preoccupation with artistic problems led him to concentrate on them to the exclusion of almost all else, an attitude apparently not uncommon in his native country. Fromentin has already remarked on it in his *Maîtres d'autrefois*. Abroad, Holland was engaged in wars throughout the seventeenth century—with Spain, with England, with the France of Louis XIV; at home, she was torn apart by fierce civil disputes and bitter quarrels in the field of religion and philosophy. Her artists seemed to notice none of this; at least, they normally made no reference to it in their work.

There is nothing very odd about such behaviour when one considers how seldom artists of other nations and other ages have chosen contemporary events for their subject-matter (except, of course, for the chroniclers, and those painters who recorded the advance of armies like present-day war correspondents). Velazquez' *Surrender of Breda* is an exception in his work, and it has no equivalent in the paintings of Titian, Tintoretto or Poussin. Even Rubens, who was entrusted with various diplomatic missions, gives no hint in his paintings of his political activities. Indeed, so foreign is his art to the history of his own country in the seventeenth century that he not only fails to reflect her trials but makes his audience forget them.

Yet however artists may try to exclude current affairs from their work, it is difficult to ignore them completely in everyday life; it is quite impossible, in fact, to escape from some of their effects. An inhabitant of seventeenth-century Holland might take an interest in his country's struggle with Spain, or he might choose to regard it with indifference, but the results of this struggle concerned him as much as anyone else. Dutch independence was a reality which could not be ignored, affecting as it did not only the institutions and organization of the state, but also the ways of life and attitudes of mind of all its citizens. By breaking the bonds which tied her to Spain and becoming a Calvinist nation, Holland cut herself off from the Catholic world. The consequences of this rupture were particularly decisive for painters and sculptors.

From the start of the modern era, the fate of Western art and that of the Catholic Church had been closely linked. During the Middle Ages it was the Church that provided artists with nearly all their commissions and subjects. They decorated religious buildings and illustrated the Church's teaching in miniatures, stained glass, paintings, tapestries and sculpture. Even the spread of new ideas introduced by the Renaissance made no significant difference to these relations. The Church kept on commissioning new works, artists went on producing large-scale treatments of religious subjects. The establishment of Calvinism, which refused to harbour in its temples the painted, sculptured images that adorned Catholic churches, meant that the demand for religious paintings in Holland was now reduced to those commissioned by private individuals who liked to have them in their own homes. In other words, religious art became something of a rarity, and the dimensions of religious paintings diminished.

There was another type of subject not greatly appreciated by Dutch clients—themes from ancient history and mythology. These were dear to princes, aristocrats and humanists, in short, to all those who cultivated (or made a pretence of cultivating) their minds. In Holland, however, painters were henceforth to rely for most of their custom on the middle class, whose members were more enterprising than cultured, more attracted by the immediate and tangible than the distant and imaginary. The favourite paintings of the Dutch bourgeois were of subjects borrowed from his own everyday life, subjects which revealed the identity and way of life of his own class and the distinguishing characteristics of his country. In other words, the artist's prime function was to paint portraits. He was also called upon to give an account of events in and around the house, to show the mother looking after home or child, the girl reading a letter or taking a music lesson, the young woman playing the lute or the harpsichord. He would be invited to portray people chatting or enjoying themselves, eating and drinking, laughing, shouting, and gesticulating—for amusement was

17

4 *Hals, Frans. Portrait of N. Hasselaer*   5 *Metsu, Gabriel. Amateur Musicians*

6 *Heda, Willem Claeszoon. Still Life*

7 van Goyen, Jan.
Landscape with River

8 Berckheyde, Job.
Interior of the
Great Church at Haarlem

not always a genteel thing confined to well-kept rooms, it could also be found in more vulgar form in smoky, crudely furnished taverns with boorish jokes and pungent smells.

The artist's customer also liked him to represent on canvas the features of the town where he lived. He liked to be able to recognize a street, the façade of a civic building, or the interior of a church. He also liked to rediscover scenes from the countryside—the land furrowed by canals, boats on the water, beasts in the fields, trees, and skies with clouds drifting from the sea. Finally, he liked the artist's brush to dwell on simple, inanimate objects—flowers and shells, glasses and pewter mugs, pies, fruit, and dead fish. The artist was required to paint all these objects in straightforward style, but he was also allowed to invest them with some symbolical significance—by adding a human skull, for instance.

Although none of these subjects was either novel or peculiar to Dutch painting, Dutch artists conferred on them an importance which no other school had ever previously contemplated. Furthermore, a Dutch painter, whether executing a portrait, genre scene, landscape or still-life, treated his subject in the manner most fitting to Holland. This style of painting can only be described as realism. It is true that realism of a kind had already made its appearance in other countries, but the Dutch variety was more open, direct, and restrained.

There can be no doubt that all the original aspects of this realism were exclusively Dutch—its characteristic features did not emerge until independence had been achieved. Only after that date did a truly Dutch style of painting come into being. As a general rule the art produced in the Northern provinces had previously borne a very close resemblance to that of the Southern Netherlands—so much so, in fact, that artists like Hieronymus Bosch and Pieter Aertsen can figure in histories of both Flemish and Dutch painting.

Even when Rembrandt was beginning to produce his first pictures, the characteristics of the Dutch school were still not clearly defined. But the lines along which it was later to develop had been established, and each branch of painting boasted artists of undeniable stature. In the realm of portraiture, Frans Hals reigned supreme. Hals was the most powerful and most modern painter of the generation which preceded Rembrandt's. There may not be much deep psychology in his work, but he portrays with great naturalism the middle-class woman in her Sunday best, the burgomaster swollen by a sense of his own importance, the ribald merrymakers, the annual banquet of this or that guild, whose officers are dressed up in old militiamen's uniforms in an effort to convince themselves that they are something more than inoffensive bourgeois worthies. What zest and fire he puts into the sweeping strokes that bring before our eyes all these characters, so common in themselves, but made noble by the beauty of the painting! Hals settled in Haarlem, but was born in either Antwerp or Malines. His Flemish origins were perhaps responsible for the vigour of his execution and the pungency of his brush-work, while he owed his restrained use of colours and realist emphasis to his adopted country.

Adriaen Brouwer, the artist who did most to create a new genre painting, was another Fleming. He was resident in Holland from 1626 to 1631, first in Amsterdam and later in Haarlem. During his early career, Brouwer had come under the influence of Pieter Bruegel, but a period spent working with Hals led him to abandon geometrical design and flat tints in favour of a more direct expression and a more specifically pictorial style. Rembrandt was later to buy some of Brouwer's paintings—less, probably, through any particular feeling of interest in their subjects, the drunken brawls of card-playing peasants, than because he was receptive to the pathos of their figures and their atmosphere.

Rembrandt also had a favourite among landscape-painters, Hercules Seghers, some of whose works he also acquired. Born in Haarlem some fifteen years before Rembrandt, Seghers preserved a liking for imaginary landscapes compounded of features drawn from different parts of the country, but he managed to give these compositions a moving reality by suffusing them with the troubled light of his own soul. His painting was not, therefore, far removed from that of Brouwer, and Rembrandt doubtless admired both artists for the same reasons.

Holland already possessed other landscape-painters, however, whose method was to record scenes as they actually saw them. The most advanced of them was Jan van Goyen, a delicate observer of the effects of light and atmosphere on sky and water. Leyden was also van Goyen's home town, and he was living there when Rembrandt returned from Amsterdam. The two artists may have come into contact with each other, but Rembrandt does not appear to have been very impressed by van Goyen's work, or strongly attracted to landscape-painting at that time. His main teacher had been a history painter, and his own inclination made him most interested in human beings. It was therefore natural that he also should want to do history painting.

CHAPTER THREE

Early compositions

For Rembrandt history meant, above all, religious history. Yet it was to ancient Greece and Rome that he sometimes turned, and which, in fact, provided him with the subject for one of his first paintings. At least, so it appears, for the meaning of the work is so unclear that it has received half a dozen different interpretations. But whether we choose to see in it *The Justice of Brutus* or *The Clemency of Emperor Titus*, whether the central character is Coriolanus, the Consul Cerialis, or someone quite different, of one thing there can be no doubt—Rembrandt experienced extreme difficulty in grouping his heroes and giving them reasonably natural attitudes. The painting has other shortcomings: the heads are badly joined to the bodies, the colours of the faces fail to tone in with those of the costumes, the characters in the background are too indistinct and do not tie up with the figures in the foreground which are drawn with excessive attention to detail. Finally, the general harmony of the tints is so unsound as to present an almost mottled impression.

Rembrandt hardly felt more at ease when he painted *The Angel and the Prophet Balaam* (1626), and the way in which the young artist tells his story still fails to carry much conviction. The angel which, *Ill. 9* in the Bible, stood in the way of the prophet's ass is here placed behind the animal. The ass is thus quite unable to see the angel, particularly as it is on its knees with its head pointing in the opposite direction. Yet however improbably the picture may be composed, it has more to it than mere clumsiness. It shows a laudable concern, which was to remain characteristic of Rembrandt's work, to capture the action at its climax. In this case the decisive moment is clearly when the ass opens its mouth and speaks. This same concern explains the gestures of Balaam and the angel, for there is a theatrical expressiveness about them which contrasts curiously with the exaggerated aloofness of the two servants on horseback as they view this agitated scene.

Rembrandt acquired his taste for gesticulation from Lastman, to whom he also owed his meticulous rendering of material objects and his rather hard, almost sculptural shapes. Rembrandt must certainly have paid close attention to Lastman's teaching—in *Balaam* even the plants in the right-hand corner with the crisp outline of their large leaves reveal his master's influence. For all that, the spiritual stresses suggested by the prophet's face enable us to catch a glimpse of Rembrandt's original qualities.

Ill. 10 A clearer indication of his originality is given by a small painting of the same year called *Tobit and Anna with the Kid*. In this picture, Rembrandt limits the number of characters to two, and confines them to a corner of their room. The face of each is made to tally with the role he plays in the Bible—Tobit deep in prayer, Anna bristling with indignation that he should think the goat she holds in her arms is stolen. Admittedly the manner in which Tobit presses his hands together is rather affected, and the expression on his face rather melodramatic. Admittedly, too, Rembrandt still records his scene in meticulous detail, the clothes of the characters and the objects in the room look as though they were made of plaster, and certain details betray a love of the picturesque and the merely anecdotal. Nevertheless, he brings out the main points and shows signs of understanding the possibilities of light. In addition, his colouring, though still fairly patchy, is both more sensitive and more harmonious than in *The Clemency of Emperor Titus*.

It was also in 1626 that Rembrandt painted his *Group of Musicians*. It shows two men, one playing the harp and the other the cello, beside two women, one singing and the other, older woman listening. The models for this picture were his mother, himself, and probably one of his sisters, together with one of his brothers or his father. Can this therefore be described as a genre painting? Certainly, genre painters portrayed similar scenes; analogies can be found in the work of Terbrugghen, Honthorst, and the Caravaggians of Utrecht, whom Rembrandt also recalls by his lighting and his arrangement of light and shade.

Yet Rembrandt's painting has a gravity, not to say solemnity, about it which sets him apart from his predecessors. There is realism in his observation of detail, but the picture also has an unreal aspect, resulting from the dress of his characters, which has nothing in common with genre painting. His turban and his drooping moustache give the cellist an oriental look; the harpist wears a slashed hat decorated with feathers; the diadem which crowns the lady singer's hair is thoroughly theatrical; the mother's head is swathed in a cap similar to the one worn by Anna, Tobit's wife.

This desire to break away from everyday reality was, and would remain, one of Rembrandt's distinguishing characteristics—at least, as far as his painting was concerned. It was for this reason that he was henceforth to eliminate from his pictures subjects typical of genre painting (that is, if one discounts his *Money-Changer* of 1627, perhaps intended as a study of avarice, and his *Foot Operation* of 1628, which he may have meant to evoke the sense of touch). This did not prevent him from making use of objects portrayed by genre painters, or indeed by still-life painters.

In fact, still-life objects figure in the foreground of various early Rembrandt paintings. *The Clemency of Emperor Titus* includes a shield, a breast-plate, and spear-heads, the *Foot Operation* an old shoe and a basket, and *The Musicians* a lute and some large books. Piles of books are also to be seen on the table of *The Money-Changer,* and similarly on the bed of *St Paul in Prison* (1627). Rembrandt *Ill. 11* paints these objects with great thoroughness, devoting hardly less attention to them than to his characters.

St Paul in Prison is one of Rembrandt's most successful paintings of this period, although Caravaggio's influence is very much in evidence. It can be observed not only in the important role of chiaroscuro but also in the fact that one of the saint's feet is bare—the Italian master's fondness for drawing attention to large, bare, dusty feet in some of

9 *The Angel and the Prophet Balaam.* 1626

10 *Tobit and Anna with the Kid.* 1626 ▷

his works is well-known. Features of Rembrandt's early work which reappear in this painting are his search for expressive postures and gestures, and his desire to emphasize the message they are to convey. St Paul is deep in thought, and to bring home to his audience that this really is so, Rembrandt shows the saint with his hand over his mouth.

St Paul's prison cell is lit by the daylight which streams through the grating window, the light in the *Money-Changer's* room comes from a candle, and in *Flight into Egypt* (1627) from the moon (its artistic source in this painting was no doubt Elsheimer, who liked to paint small nocturnal landscapes). Right from the start, then, Rembrandt was bringing different lighting effects into play, studying the various qualities that light can possess and the different effects it is capable of producing. But, for the time being, he did no more than project shafts of light on to objects, illuminating the surface, but not yet transfiguring them. Rembrandt's use of light was only to lose its superficiality when he abandoned sharp definition, paid less attention to filling out the bodies of his characters, and restrained his colouring which, under Lastman's influence, had hitherto been rather bright and varied. He began to make these modifications to his style around 1628, and it comes as no surprise that he first achieved his objective in small canvases. One such picture portrays *A Painter in his Studio.* Whether the painter in question is Rembrandt himself or his pupil Gerard Dou is of only minor importance. What counts is the composition and style of the work.

The artist can be seen standing at the back of his studio, his size reduced by the distance. An empty space separates him from the easel which looms up in the foreground, its dark shadow cast across the floor by the back-lighting. Apart from the blue of the painter's dressing-gown, the colouring fluctuates between light grey and dark brown. This new restraint in Rembrandt's use of colours is complemented by a reduction of anecdotal elements. In this respect, it is interesting to compare the picture to a similar work produced at the same period by Gerard Dou. In Dou's painting, the artist, this time unquestionably Rembrandt, stands more to the foreground and also closer to the easel, which is now shown not from the back but from the front, thus revealing the picture to which the artist is preparing to apply the finishing touches. Furthermore, the studio is littered with objects that distract the attention—some lying about on the floor,

11 *St Paul in Prison.* 1627

some hanging from the wall, still others standing on a table in the background. Behind the painter is an open door, through which a man may be seen entering—an art-lover, no doubt. By dwelling on all these picturesque details, Dou provides a minute account of how Rembrandt's studio may have appeared on a certain day.

Rembrandt's treatment of the subject reveals something quite different. Of course, he does not picture the studio as an abstract or anonymous environment, and he consequently displays certain special features of the floor, the wood of the door (which in his version stays shut), and the cracks in the wall. He also places a table and some objects behind the artist, although these are hardly noticeable, and has a palette hanging up on the wall in the background (Dou reproduces a portrait in this position). But Rembrandt is most concerned, not with the objects in themselves, but with the relationship which exists between them: firstly, the vibrations of the light and the dialogue between light and shade; secondly, tensions of a psychological kind. On the one hand there is the painter, thick-set, determined and uneasy; on the other there is the easel, its vast expanse of canvas flooded with a pitiless light, provocative, assertive, stimulating, at times driving one to despair. From the troubled mind and insignificant body of the artist thus emerges the luminous and impressive evidence of a work of art. The painting is an evocation of the creative act.

It must be admitted, however, that the contrast between the huge dimensions of the canvas on the easel and the artist's own diminutive stature is overdone in the same theatrical manner already remarked upon above—a fault to be found in almost all Rembrandt's youthful works. Rembrandt's habit of emphasizing the effects he wished to make had probably been instilled by Lastman, but no doubt a desire that his work should be immediately intelligible also helps to explain it.

After all, it was the very aspects of *Judas returning the Thirty Pieces of Silver* which seem theatrical to modern eyes that aroused Constantijn Huygens' enthusiasm. In *The Raising of Lazarus*, Christ is depicted in an even more spectacular pose than Judas. A brilliant light strikes the raised arm, instantly capturing the attention and leading the eye along the majestic vertical which extends right down to the edge of the tomb and the pallid figure of Lazarus. In this work, the light fulfils the sole purpose of illustrating what the artist wishes to say. Thus Rembrandt applies light colours at the points where the desired effect demands it, vindicating them by an arm, a face, a neck, a shroud, or the quiver and sword which he hangs over the grave, without asking himself whether or not they are relevant to his subject.

It was probably shortly before painting this picture that Rembrandt produced one of his finest works of this period, *Christ at Emmaus* (c. 1629). There is an undeniable recurrence of exaggerated pathos in the way in which Christ draws himself up to break the bread, as also in the attitudes of his two disciples—the one sits opposite him, shocked and afraid, the other has thrown himself in confusion at Christ's feet. Nevertheless, the general effect of this work is nothing less than admirable—this because of the lighting, which speaks more eloquently than the postures of the characters, and indicates far better than they that we are witnessing something unbelievable, something miraculous. Back-lighting may again intrude, as in *A Painter in his Studio,* but here it fulfils a far more expressive purpose. It makes the figures in the foreground almost incorporeal, stripping them of their ordinary, physical existence. The distribution of light and shade is such that two-thirds of the painting is covered in darkness. In the background, this would risk becoming impenetrable were it not for the woman bustling about by a blazing hearth. The other source of light is hidden by Christ, so that one can see only the rays issuing from it, an arrangement which gives the light a mysterious, spiritual quality.

Though the absence of back-lighting in *Jeremiah lamenting the Destruction of Jerusalem* might suggest that Rembrandt had abandoned it in 1630, he did not similarly neglect the material aspect of objects; he went to great pains, for instance, to reconstruct the characteristic look, and even feel, of various materials. A backward glance, however, is enough to demonstrate how far Rembrandt's art had come since 1626. The change lies not in the high value which he sets on beautiful fabrics, but in the sensitivity with which he treats them. His brush touches them and weighs them with greater finesse, and records far more skilfully the exquisite sensations they gave him. In addition, light is coming to play an increasingly important part in his work. Whereas, originally, light served the purposes of the narrative and the delineation of shapes, it is now emerging as a feature in its own right.

Nothing illustrates this and other changes better than a comparison between his two separate versions of *The Presentation in the Temple.*

12 *The Presentation in the Temple.* About 1628

13 *The Presentation in the Temple.* 1631

Ill. 12   His first attempt at this subject, executed around 1628, contains five characters—the old man Simeon and the child, the Virgin and St Joseph, and the prophetess Anna. All of them are large in relation to the size of the painting. They are seen from close up, and the details of their clothing are readily distinguishable. Together the group forms a pyramid, and the general massiveness of the effect is heightened by the huge pillar behind them. Their gestures, especially that of the prophetess, still possess the theatrical quality already encountered on previous occasions. The technique is painstaking and laborious, and the general effect fails to generate much feeling.

Ill. 13   In contrast, the second version of *The Presentation in the Temple*, painted in 1631, sets the scene in an immense space, a temple of grand proportions, and a number of other figures have now been added. The central characters in the episode, though situated further away, are more imposing than in the first version. The high priest, draped in a full purple robe, embodies a grave dignity. His gesture is solemn without being overemphatic. The solemnity of the moment is accentuated by the light, which leaves everything but the central group in semi-darkness, and falls full on the child and the old man Simeon, the characters who most need to stand out. Apart from this, the treatment has lost its over-insistent character, and the colouring has become sparser and less sharply defined. In short, Rembrandt shows himself to be more assured and more profound in every respect.

34

CHAPTER FOUR

Deciphering the human face

During his Leyden period, Rembrandt painted more than just compositions. His curiosity was inflamed by the human face, which he wished to examine and interpret in paintings entirely devoted to it. This he did in a series of pictures of generally rather small dimensions in which the head, or the upper half of the body are the only features of his characters to appear.

The models he used were usually his mother, and either his father or an old man of unknown identity. All these were old people. Nothing excited the young painter more, indeed, than the faces of those who had lived to old age. He was fascinated by skins tanned, wrinkled and furrowed by time, lips thinned or flattened by the passage of years, corners of mouths marked by the bitter taste of stubborn, exhausting effort. As expressiveness often meant more to him than verisimilitude, Rembrandt thought nothing of getting his models to dress up in the clothes of a vain mercenary, or of an old officer of stern expression: he would drape gold chains round their shoulders and set plumed hats on their heads. In his mother's case, Rembrandt took pleasure in turning her into a prophetess, portraying her in a succession of attitudes—thoughtful, in prayer, leaning on a

Ill. 14

35

14 *Rembrandt's Mother as the Prophetess Anna.* 1631

bible. He always hoped to find in the faces of those who posed for him a fresh insight into the human condition, for the important thing as far as Rembrandt was concerned was not beauty but truth. He far preferred an ugliness that moved him to an attractive prettiness. The same attitude could be found in the works of other contemporary artists. Numerous paintings of the time featured old men, and in many instances these portraits were inspired by Caravaggio's example.

As well as faces whose features had become hollowed and hardened with age, however, Rembrandt also portrayed faces which time had not yet deeply marked. For almost all these studies Rembrandt relied on a single model—himself. Indeed, he was never to grow tired of executing self-portraits. The latest catalogue of his paintings, just published by Kurt Bauch, reproduces no less than fifty-six, about fifteen of which date from his Leyden period alone. This is without mentioning his drawings and etchings.

Why did Rembrandt portray himself so often? It was not through any narcissistic love of his own face, or because he believed himself to have a particularly handsome body. Rather, he saw in his face an object of study which would at all times lend itself submissively to his exploration. This accounts for the fact that his self-portraits are so varied—they differ not only in the range of feelings which he uses them to express but also in the variations of clothing and lighting. No analysis of the meaning of these works should lose sight of the fact that some of the faces portrayed are little more than masks. This is not due to any lack of sincerity or wish for self-concealment on the part of the artist. Rembrandt rather considered himself as an actor called upon to play a variety of roles. Hence his face and his demeanour are very often to be explained less in terms of his real nature than of the appearance he wished to assume. Of course, the very fact that Rembrandt should have liked to play all these parts, and dress himself up in various forms of fancy dress is not without significance. But by far the most important motivating factor was a wish to get to know the resources of expression in his own face.

Here is how he drew himself about 1629: a young, bearish peasant, headstrong, obstinate, unsociable, a little surly even; eyes which gaze steadily at their target; untidy hair with wisps licking round his head like flames, and no attempt at style—in fact an out-and-out rejection of style, the hair of a rebel; most definitely not a man who aims to

15 *Self-portrait.* 1629

please. How faithfully does this image reproduce the real Rembrandt?
Other portraits of the same period give the impression that Rembrandt here set out to make himself look older. No doubt he also affected to be more assured and more intractable than he actually was.

Ill. 15 At any rate, his features are gentler and more youthful in other studies of the time. In the *Self-Portrait* housed in the Alte Pinakothek, Munich (1629), his face could almost be that of a child wishing to make a surreptitious entry into the world, and approaching it with a questioning look and a greedy, vulnerable mouth. The highly

16 *Self-portrait.* 1629

arbitrary lighting falls full on his cheek, making the fleshy nose stand out while the eyes and that part of the forehead not covered by his still unkempt hair are left in shadow.

Although it was painted in the same year, the *Self-Portrait* which hangs in the Mauritshuis, The Hague, reveals another face again. This *Ill. 16* time we are confronted with a young man who knows his own worth and would like everybody else to recognize it too. Rembrandt here wears a gorget and a fine muslin collar. His hair is still long, but some care has now gone into arranging it. A strong, stubborn will can be discerned in the way he holds his head, as also in the furrow which runs down his brow towards his nose. For all his prepossessing air he is clearly anxious to assert himself—but the pose is obvious. The free play of chiaroscuro in the previous work is not here repeated; its function is simply to accentuate the dignity of the character, not to give a display of the artist's imagination. The execution is carefully done, and the paint smooth and transparent. This was a deferential work executed with the public in mind, a picture which proclaimed that Rembrandt was capable of producing portraits which would give his models no cause for complaint.

The self-confident expression he bears in this work is replaced elsewhere by uneasiness and surliness. He may also be seen with his mouth open, apparently stammering, or with his face distorted by a forced and rather silly laugh. In one full-length portrait he even gives himself the appearance of an oriental prince; smothered in rich robes, a thin moustache on his arrogant face, he plants himself before us leaning on a walking stick which he holds in his gloved left hand, while an idiotic poodle sits at his feet. It is hard to tell what kind of impression he hoped to create with an image so grotesque that even he must have smiled to look at it. On the other hand, he was certainly never reluctant to push himself forward. One sometimes imagines that he wished to say to his fellow-countrymen: 'Look at me, I may be only a miller's son, but I appreciate fine clothes! When I'm dressed like this, I'm as distinguished as any man.'

CHAPTER FIVE

First drawings and etchings

An appreciation of Rembrandt which merely confined itself to his paintings would neglect an essential aspect of his work. For he also left a considerable number of etchings and drawings, many of which differ from his paintings in both subject-matter and style. Rembrandt used a variety of methods and materials: red and black chalk, pen and brush for his drawings, nitric acid and at times drypoint for his etchings. Understandably, he was not attracted by the engraver's burin. Seventeenth-century artists in general preferred the etching-needle, which enabled them to draw as freely on the varnish-covered surface of the copper-plate as with a pencil on a sheet of paper. The parts of the plate laid bare by the movement of the needle were bitten by the etching acid, so that grooves of varying widths and depths were scored in the metal. In the printing, this would produce thin or thick lines, soft greys or sombre blacks, as the case might be. Rembrandt was even more inclined to use nitric acid in that he was a painter—one indeed who strove especially for painterly effects and whose essential method was not the sharp outline, but the play of gradations and the effects of light and shade. Besides, Rembrandt liked to draw in quick, irregular, almost whimsical strokes, a technique which the burin did not allow.

17 *Rembrandt's Father.* 1630   18 *Rembrandt's Mother with her Hand on her Breast.* 1631

The date which appears on Rembrandt's earliest prints is 1628. He must have produced others prior to that, however, as these prints are undeniably the work of a man who knows his trade. He is thought to have been initiated into the art by Lievens. To judge from the works which have come down to us, Rembrandt's first etchings were portraits. For these he used the same models as in his paintings—his *Ills 17, 18* mother, his father, an unidentified old man, and finally himself, once more trying to detect new expressions in a face, which varied between sternness and a sneering laugh, calm dignity and haughty defiance. These works are mostly small in size, often they measure no more than 8 centimetres either way. But the execution is lively, the features of the faces are described in great detail, an impression of depth is successfully created, and one can almost feel the skin of the subject and the texture of the materials.

Other prints of this period feature beggars. The idea of portraying them probably came from Callot, whose works were circulating in Holland at that time. Rembrandt himself was later to purchase some, though exactly when he did so is not known. In any event, Rem-

42

19 *Crippled Beggar.* About 1630

brandt's beggars, with their emaciated faces and the sticks and crutches on which they invariably lean to walk, are observed with greater feeling than Callot's and unlike the French artist, Rembrandt does not disguise the fact that the dubious picturesqueness of their rags conceals a genuine misery *(Crippled Beggar).* His style also differs from   *Ill. 19* Callot's. His strokes are light and free; at certain points one is

43

20 *Large Standing Beggar.* About 1630

tempted to say that he lets them wander. Rembrandt suggests rather than describes.

However, the most significant and original works which Rembrandt produced in black and white during this period were studies of naked women. He drew them and also, around 1630, made them the subject of two etchings. The prints accentuate a feature already apparent in

21 *The blind Fiddler.* 1631

22 *The Leper.* 1629

23 Naked Woman seated on a Mound. 1631

the drawings—a resolute, almost aggressive refusal on Rembrandt's part to idealize his figures in any way. These bodies have no vestige of charm about them; they lack even the lure which can sometimes be imparted to ungraceful flesh by an allusion to vice. Rembrandt's *Naked Woman sitting on a Mound* has a heavy belly which sags down on to her thighs, fleshy hips, and rolls of fat under her breasts and around her knees. Among the works of Rembrandt's predecessors one would search in vain, not perhaps for similar realism, but certainly for such an eagerness to display ugliness.

Ill. 23

46

24 *Seated naked Woman.* 1630

Other artists had of course used ugliness before Rembrandt. One thinks of Michelangelo's *Night* with that belly marred by a mass of folds, or the nudes in Dürer's *Women bathing* and *Four Witches.* Yet in these cases ugliness is to some extent softened by other factors— in Michelangelo's work the woman has something heroic about her, for she seems to belong to a superhuman race; Dürer is clearly concerned to bring out the contrast between his inharmonious nudes and a body nearing the ideal formulated by the Italian Renaissance.

Nothing of the kind appears in Rembrandt's work. For him, this

47

woman is neither a mythical being, nor is the function of her ugliness to emphasize the beauty of perfect proportions. Nor is she even a symbol of moral bankruptcy. Rembrandt's aim is not to denounce or to vindicate ugliness. He simply states that it exists, that it is one of the facts of life, and that, as such, it is no less deserving of our fervent attention than beauty.

CHAPTER SIX

Fame and happiness

Of all the portraits which Rembrandt painted in 1631, two stand out
from the rest; firstly because of their rather large dimensions, and
secondly because of the appearance of the characters. Unlike other
early works, they were not studies in expression or in exotic clothing,
but faithful portraits which were certainly painted on commission.
The two men portrayed are Nicolaes Ruts, an Amsterdam merchant;
and a scholar who was once thought to be the writing-master Lieven
van Coppenol. Each is shown with the expression which he puts on
when he wishes to appear respectable, and with the clothes he wears
to go out on Sundays. This costume is difficult to reconcile with the
attitude and profession of the scholar, as he sits in front of a weighty
book with a pen in his hand, but far from being worried by this
inconsistency the character was probably delighted with the result.
The portrait displays two things which he liked to show were worthy
of respect—his impeccable dress, and his position in society. As a
general rule, Rembrandt aimed to satisfy his sitters, denying himself
the least whim and treating them with all the consideration they
could want.

Who was it that recommended them to go to Rembrandt in the first place? The answer is suggested by a document, dated 20 June 1631, in which Hendrick van Uylenburgh, an Amsterdam art dealer, acknowledged that he owed Rembrandt the sum of 1000 guilders. A debt of this importance presupposes that relations between artist and dealer had already existed for some years, for the young painter's prices cannot have been very high. In all propability then, van Uylenburgh was the intermediary through whom Rembrandt's works, and in particular his etchings, were sold in Amsterdam. Again, it was probably thanks to him that Rembrandt's reputation spread in the capital and that he received certain commissions for portraits. Finally, when Rembrandt decided to settle in Amsterdam towards the end 1631, it was at van Uylenburgh's house that he stayed.

It is not surprising that Rembrandt should have wished to change his place of residence. Although Leyden was the second largest town in Holland, its population was less than half that of Amsterdam. Amsterdam was also the largest port in the country, and its main centre of trade. Due to the activities of the Dutch East India Company and the Dutch West India Company it received a heavy flow of produce from places as far apart as Indonesia, Brazil, Australia and

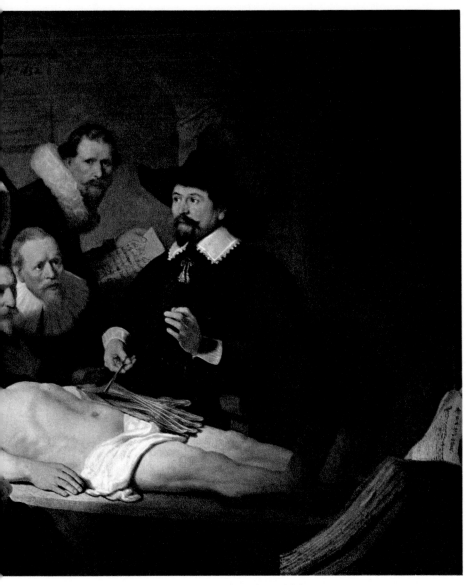

25 *The Anatomy Lesson of Professor Tulp.* 1632

South Africa. Descartes, writing to Guez de Balzac in 1631, said: 'You must excuse my zeal if I invite you to choose Amsterdam for your retirement, and to prefer it not only to all the Capuchin and Carthusian monasteries, to which many worthy people retire, but also to the finest residences in France and Italy, and even to the famous hermitage where you lived last year. However well-organized a house in the country may be, it always lacks an infinite number of commodities which can be found only in towns, while even the solitude one hopes to find there is never complete. . . . No doubt there is a pleasure to be derived from watching the fruit in your orchards grow in great abundance, but do you imagine one cannot see at least as much here in Amsterdam, unloaded by the vessels that bring us such a copious supply of everything produced in the Indies and all that is rare in Europe? Which other place in the whole world could one choose where all the commodities of life are so easy to find as in Amsterdam?' Amsterdam, in short, was a wealthy, cosmopolitan city where an artist would naturally feel more stimulated and find a wider range of possibilities than in Leyden.

No doubt Rembrandt settled there with the firm intention of taking advantage of all the opportunities he might be offered. Fate was kind to him, for as early as 1632 he obtained a commission which contributed substantially to his reputation. He was invited to paint an *Anatomy Lesson* which Professor Nicolaes Tulp was to give his pupils, using a man's corpse. In other words, Rembrandt had to execute one of those group portraits of which the Dutch were so fond.

Ill. 25

Already in the sixteenth century, the custom had sprung up among fraternities, corporations, militia companies, and governors and governesses of charitable institutions of having themselves portrayed at their meetings or banquets. The problem they thus posed to painters was not easily solved, for there was a fundamental contradiction about this kind of picture. The artist was required to provide a faithful portrait of each member of the group, and to lavish the same amount of attention on each face. He was thus obliged to show all the characters (or almost all) facing in the same direction, towards the front, which made it difficult to convey the impression that they were really involved in an action. For instance, Thomas de Keyser's painting of *The Anatomy Lesson of Dr Sebastian Egbertsz* (1619) fails to convince the onlooker that something really is happening, or at least

26 The Standard-Bearer. 1635

that there is a plausible relationship between the sitters and the human skeleton which stands in their midst. The lecturer, who sits in the foreground, is making a set gesture whose meaning remains obscure. The student opposite him is looking towards the spectator rather as one would face a camera today. Another student is pretending to take an interest in the skeleton, but he, like his colleagues, appears to find it more amusing than instructive.

In order to create a natural relationship between the characters and the object of their study, Rembrandt groups them round the corpse, which he extends slightly to the side in the foreground. Further, he chooses to paint the moment when everyone's attention is captured by the same thing—the muscles and tendons of arm and hand which Professor Tulp has just exposed with his scissors. This exploration of the structure of the human body is no longer something we find particularly exciting, but at that time dissection had only just been authorized in the Netherlands (it could only be practised on the corpses of criminals), and anatomy was a science in which not only doctors but also ordinary laymen took an interest—so much so, in fact, that classes in anatomy for the general public were begun even in non-university towns. Does Rembrandt's painting convey an idea of the interest which anatomical studies aroused?

The lecturer is as solemn as one could wish for. He could hardly be more conscious of the importance of his profession, as he stands in a rather stiff pose with the air of a teacher pronouncing incontrovertible discoveries. As for Tulp's seven students, two or three of them appear to be paying attention (one leans over the pale corpse, watching with rather exaggerated curiosity), but the majority are less concerned with the anatomy and their instructor's explanations than with the appearance which they present to the onlooker. They could just as easily look the same in a work which treated an altogether different subject. Although Rembrandt contrives to make his painting less formal than de Keyser's, he too fails to avoid all the pitfalls of this kind of picture.

The individual portraits cannot be termed particularly striking, or the characterization of the sitters very forceful. The concentration which can be read in the features of the best-observed characters has the effect of presenting a merely momentary expression, thereby denying us much insight into the workings of their minds. As far as the pictorial qualities of the work are concerned, there are some parts which are remarkably well-done (especially Professor Tulp), while other sections are executed skilfully, but without much feeling. The group has unity—a little too much, in fact. One notices rather too quickly what it is based upon—two juxtaposed pyramids, one formed by the lecturer, the other by the central group of students. It is also a little too obvious that the function of the two students placed outside the pyramid is to disguise the over-simple, monotonous effect created by the same geometrical figure being repeated.

Yet it must not be forgotten that Rembrandt was still only in his early stages as a painter, and that the problem be had to solve was a particularly thankless one. Even if *The Anatomy Lesson of Professor Tulp* cannot be classed as one of his most moving creations, it is a work of importance both in the history of the group portrait and in the artist's own career. It is easy to understand the impact which it made on the Dutch public, and the fame which it brought a painter of only 25—a fame which naturally won him other commissions for portraits, so that before long he had become the most esteemed portraitist in Amsterdam.

Many people in Amsterdam at that time were eager for their image to be perpetuated on canvas by the artist's brush, for a number of factors combined to give the Dutch bourgeois a sense of his own importance: the independence achieved through such bravery and tenacity; the nation's daily increasing power, its prosperity, growing at a similar rate; and finally Calvinism, which brought each individual into direct contact with God. All these considerations made the middle classes set a high value on the portrait.

Rembrandt thus entertained a flow of clients—merchants, craftsmen, burgomasters and pastors. The painter Jacques de Gheyn and the Secretary to the Council of State Maurits Huygens, brother of Constantijn, also came to his studio. Rembrandt's models often brought their wives along with them, but only very occasionally did husband and wife pose together for the same picture. When a couple did express a wish to be painted side by side, or a parent next to one of his children, the artist hardly bothered to show the special realationship which existed between them. It is exceptional to witness a little scene of intimacy, as in *The Shipbuilder and his Wife* (1633). The shipbuilder sits in his study, a compass in his hand and a sheet of

27 *Rembrandt and Saskia at Table.* About 1635

28 *Saskia in Profile.* 1633

paper with drawings in front of him, and his wife has come in and interrupted him for a moment to hand him a note.

In the other portraits, which constitute the great majority, Rembrandt's client had a choice between various formulae, and the selection of one rather than the other can probably be explained by the amount he agreed to spend. Thus sometimes only the upper half of the body can be seen, sometimes the hands as well, while on other occasions the portrait is full-length, showing the model either seated or standing. Invariably, the sitter wears a serious expression and stares straight in front of him. Invariably, he is dressed in black or grey, and his face emerges from a white ruff or a lace collar. He has only one concern—to be looked upon as a worthy citizen of Calvinist, commercial Holland. He never asks the artist to idealize him or to impart an exciting inner life, he merely requires that his respectability be brought out, no matter how mediocre and boring the nature which it conceals.

Rembrandt was quite prepared to fall in with this request, and he did so in the traditional manner of previous and contemporary portraitists. Rembrandt's portrait style is not far removed from that of Nicolaes Eliasz, called Pickenoy, or Michiel Jansz. van Mierevelt who, before Rembrandt arrived in Amsterdam, were providing similar clients with portraits executed with diligence and restraint. The faces Rembrandt portrays are smoothly finished, and the clothes are reproduced with care. In his use of light he certainly differs from his predecessors, for without ever allowing it completely free play he rids it of its neutral character. He lights part of the face quite vividly, and abandons the rest to transparent shadow.

Taken one by one, these portraits are not without interest, but it would be wrong to say that they all display artistic genius. Several of them are production-line paintings, and do not possess the rare qualities which can be appreciated in, for instance, the portraits of *Marten Soolmans* and his wife *Oopjen Coppit* (1634). Intellectually, these characters do not apper to have much depth or resource to them, to judge from their rather inexpressive features. The portraits are full-length, however, so the faces do not occupy much space. The main thing is the clothes, or rather the way in which the clothes are painted.

Fromentin, who wrote at a time when the sitters' names were

believed to be Maerten Daey and Machteld van Doorn, saw much to admire in these paintings, and gave a shrewd account of their merits: 'Just black, grey, and white, neither more nor less, but the tonality is peerless. The atmosphere is invisible, yet one can feel the air. The figures are modelled only slightly, but with a maximum of relief. Rembrandt has an inimitable way of being precise but not petty, of contrasting the most delicate touches with the most sweeping general effects, of using tone to express the luxury and value of objects. In a word, he displays a sureness of eye, a sensitivity of colouring, and a dexterity which would do honour to a master-painter.'

However, Rembrandt would generally become fully involved in his portraits and bring his most remarkable abilities into play only if the mind of his sitter did not leave him indifferent. For this reason Maurits Huygens, in whose look Rembrandt could detect uneasiness, inspired him more than the poet-smith Jan Hermansz. Krul, whose expression merely suggested inflated vanity. Similarly, his rendering of the foppish burgomaster Jan Pellicorn is less felicitous than his portrait of the preacher Johannes Uytenbogaert, a man with a thinker's face. He was perhaps particularly interested in Uytenbogaert because of his background—after the death of Arminius he had become the leader of the Arminians and then, when the sect was overthrown by the Gomarists in 1618—19, had been forced to flee into exile, where he remained for seven years. There is nothing to suggest that Rembrandt himself took up the cause of the Arminians, who represented the liberal wing of Calvinism, but it is probably correct to presume that he experienced some fellow-feeling for a man who had been compelled by his convictions to oppose narrow doctrines, and finally to go into exile.

Rembrandt painted some other portraits during the 1630s in which the face is more expressive than usual. The models for these pictures, which do not always seem to have been commissioned, were Jews and Orientals. What prompted him to paint them? Van Uylenburgh's house, where Rembrandt lived, was situated in the Jodenbreestraat, or Broad Street of the Jews, a name which indicates that there was a considerable Jewish community in the area. One can picture Rembrandt rubbing shoulders with them in the street, and being interested by their exotic appearance—his imagination must have been fired by the thought of the countries they came from. What is more, these

29 *Saskia as Flora.* 1634

Jews were for Rembrandt a walking illustration of the Bible. He was able to identify them with Biblical characters, and dream that he was in the presence of Abraham, Moses, the patriarchs and the prophets.

The artist in him could not always feel a slave to dull, workaday reality, he needed to let his imagination wander. There was not much to dream about in the insignificant face of a corn merchant who knew nothing but his trade. But when he looked at those broad faces inhabited by grave thoughts and framed by dignified beards, when, instead of the austere costume and black hat of his compatriots, he could paint a sparkling turban, or one of those large velvet cloaks which showed up his model's foreign origin and emphasized his venerable authority, then the elements were assembled which enabled him if not to excel himself, at least to do himself full justice. Commentators on Rembrandt's work used to take some of the characters in these portraits for rabbis. In fact, they were no doubt ordinary Jews made more splendid by his imagination—their features reappear in compositions inspired by the scriptures.

These early years in Amsterdam were thus an exciting period in Rembrandt's life. He had quickly managed to compel recognition, and had become the most sought-after portraitist in the city. He was never again in the whole of his career to have as many portrait commissions as between 1632 and 1635 and, although he worked with spirit and enthusiasm, he had difficulty in meeting all the demands made on him.

He not only sampled the headiness of success, but also the intoxication of love. He met the girl who attracted him in the very house where he was living. She was twenty years of age in 1632, and her name was Saskia van Uylenburgh. Saskia was the cousin of Hendrick, the art dealer, with whom she stayed when she came to Amsterdam. Her parents, both of whom she had lost at an early age, were Frisian aristocrats and had left each of their nine children a substantial inheritance.

There can be little doubt that Rembrandt was happy to increase his fame as an artist through a marriage which introduced him, a miller's son, into a family of such eminence. (Saskia's father had been the Burgomaster of Leeuwarden, while two of her brothers-in-law were theology professors.) He was later to scoff at the different ranks which everyone, including himself, occupied in the social scale, but

30 *Self-portrait.* 1634

31 *Self-portrait*. About 1634

it is not unlikely that, at the time, he was trying to increase his standing.

On 5 June 1633, Rembrandt and Saskia were betrothed, and a year later they celebrated their marriage. He had already introduced her into his painting in 1632. To judge from the number of pictures in which she appears, Rembrandt must have been deeply in love with her. Presumably it was her gentleness and her pleasant manner which he found so attractive, for, with her fleshy face and heavy chin, she was no great beauty. Even her smile in the famous portrait in the Gemäldegalerie, Dresden, is devoid of charm. All this mattered little, however, as Rembrandt set about displaying her to best advantage. He dressed her in a sumptuous array of clothing, set large feathered hats on her head, decked her out with necklaces, bracelets and jewels. In short, he made a lady of her. At times he even went so far as to make her into a goddess. In versions of her as *Flora* he completely transformed her, adorning her head with a crown of flowers and putting a flowered staff in her hand; at times her appearance is delicate and graceful, at others she is rather robust and over-blown. Rembrandt even portrayed her as *Bellona,* her head capped with a helmet, her body enclosed in a suit of armour and her left arm protected by an imposing shield, while her right hand holds a sword.

Ill. 27   Another painting shows Rembrandt and Saskia together. She is seated on his lap, and he rests one hand on her waist as if to signify that she really is his wife, his property. Rembrandt feels a childish need to call the whole world to witness his happiness and his pleasures. He therefore shows himself facing the spectator, a glass of wine in his raised hand and a coarse laugh on his dissipated features. Apart from that, he mounts a splendid display of velvet, valuable weapons and dishes fit for a gourmet. One has the impression that he derived a twofold pleasure from the scene; firstly, because everything in it belonged to him and, secondly, because he was able to reproduce it with such joy and skill. It is not surprising to find that Rembrandt feels more at ease in this painting than when he has to portray the colourless bourgeois of Amsterdam and their unprepossessing wives. In these portraits of Saskia, Rembrandt's art has a fullnes and flavour about it. The *Saskia* in the Gemäldegalerie, Kassel (1635), with the dull warmth of its reds, is particularly worthy of note, as is the *Saskia*
Ill. 29   *as Flora* in the Hermitage, Leningrad (1634), with its cold golds and

its greens. These are splendid pictures, in which tender feeling is allied to a delicate richness of colouring.

Rembrandt's self-portraits of this period are executed in the same *Ills 30, 31* spirit as the paintings in which he presents his wife. He is clearly anxious that they should reveal him as a man more elegant (and no less dignified) than the compatriots who asked him to paint their portraits. His hair and his moustache are arranged with care, his dress is all studied elegance. He is usually concerned to look distinguished, and dresses in velvet with a gold chain draped around his neck. On other occasions, however, he dons a warrior's helmet, or a large slashed velvet hat whose rather pompous, bizarre appearance is accentuated by the ostrich feathers. His aim is to give himself the warlike look of an enterprising officer, but all one can detect is a character of rakish self-conceit. One wonders whether this was the real Rembrandt, or whether he put on a face to match the costume. Yet nobody but he can have chosen the uniform. The inescapable evidence is that there were times when the real human being was of less importance to him than the appearance.

Rembrandt may have been moved to adopt this attitude because he believed that putting on such a pose would help him to assert his authority. He may have wished to emphasize his position in a society which did not, admittedly, dismiss painters, but which judged them to be of lesser social standing than a merchant or a ship-owner. Considerations such as these must, it seems, have contributed to determining his behaviour. Yet there is another explanation which springs to mind. Rembrandt set about showing how satisfied, wealthy and happy he was with such ostentation, and at times such arrogance, that he seems to have wished, if not to shock his compatriots, at any rate to let them know that their strict, inflexible Calvinist principles did not by any means possess the same overriding priority as far as he was concerned. When he painted such men, Rembrandt respected their taste, and allowed them their narrow-mindedness and their austere dress. But when he came to portray himself, his attitude changed completely; he broke away from rigid rules and gave himself up to freedom and fantasy.

Consequently, it comes as no surprise that Rembrandt was accused in certain quarters of throwing away his money, and in particular his wife's dowry. When this gossip was brought to his notice, Rembrandt was furious. He refused to allow such a thing to be said about him and in 1638, being apparently of a litigious nature, he sued for slander those who had claimed he was squandering Saskia's inheritance by his boastfulness and ostentation. Rembrandt's opponents denied ever having held the opinions which he reproached them with, and as a result the court dismissed his suit.

It is hard to believe that Rembrandt was really as innocent as he made himself out to be. Certainly, his portraits were bringing him in a lot of money, but all the indications are that he was spending even more. His desires were manifold, and he seems to have thought it necessary to satisfy them as far as he possibly could. His liking for helmets, shields, and breast-plates emerges from his self-portraits and the portraits of Saskia. He also liked to acquire Venetian glass, Chinese porcelain, Japanese fans, medals — and, of course, works of art. He would not hesitate to offer a high price for anything which aroused his covetousness at the public art auctions.

On one day in 1637 Rembrandt bought a set of prints by Lucas van Leyden, on another the Rubens painting *Hero and Leander* and a few months later, in 1638, some Italian etchings. He may even have bought in order to resell at a higher price. Perhaps he found a taste for business — this would not after all be very surprising in a country where trade occupied such an important position, and lay behind the quick rise to prosperity of so many citizens. ('In this great city there is no one but I who does not go in for trade', wrote Descartes in 1631.) But success in this sphere requires more than a good knowledge of the 'business'. Rembrandt would have had to devote the same amount of time and energy to commercial matters as he habitually did (and continued to do) to artistic creation. Even if he dabbled in business, he would never have been able to go in for it in a big way.

CHAPTER SEVEN

Notes in the sketchbook

When the dates of the portraits of Saskia are examined, it is apparent that the great majority were painted between 1632 and 1634. After that date they became few and far between, and for certain years (1637–40) there are none at all. The explanation for this may be that Saskia no longer had the time to pose, or that she was no longer in a fit state to do so. From the family documents it emerges that in December 1635, Saskia gave birth to a boy who was called after her father Rumbartus: he died after two months. Another child was born in July 1638, this time a girl whom they called Cornelia: she survived for little more than three weeks. A second Cornelia took her place in July 1640, but she also failed to last long. The family life of Rembrandt and his wife was thus far from being one of uninterrupted happiness, particularly as these trials had their effect not only on Saskia's mind — they also undermined her health. Although no text and no painting reveals this deterioration, the evidence in Rembrandt's drawings is quite clear.

As a general rule, Rembrandt discloses things, when he uses line-drawing or wash, which he does not express with brush and paint. In

32 *Saskia betrothed.* 1633

33 *Saskia seated by a Window.* 1633–34

the latter case, he naturally thinks that his picture will one day belong to someone else, and he anticipates the dialogue which will take place between painting and onlooker. His drawings, on the other hand, are soliloquies. He records the things which are on his mind, things which do not always concern his fellow-men. Thus, nothing in his work is more revealing than his drawings. On the one hand, they show the wide range of subjects which excited his curiosity, on the other they

34 *Saskia in Bed with a seated Woman.* About 1636

enlighten us about many aspects of his private life. As far as Saskia is concerned, they provide us with information which one might have been able to surmise, but which one would never have known with such certainty without them.

Ill. 32   On one of these drawings Rembrandt has inscribed: 'This is a portrait of my wife when she was twenty-one years of age, the third day of our betrothal, 8 June 1633'. Saskia has a confiding look on her plump, placid face. There even seems to be the suggestion of a smile

35 *Weeping Child.* About 1635

playing around her mouth. Nowhere in a painted portrait does she appear so fresh and so graceful. She wears a large hat which casts a light shadow over her forehead but which does not give her the rather too stiff appearance which she usually has in the paintings. The face is drawn slightly in relief, but elsewhere shape is evoked only by a small number of brisk strokes. The silverpoint which Rembrandt used for this portrait skims the surface of the paper at certain points and at others leaves a firm mark.

71

Ill. 33

Rembrandt turned to pen and brush a few months later to draw *Saskia seated by a Window*. In this portrait the lines are thicker, and light and darkness are sharply contrasted. Saskia's face has also changed, for although it has not lost its plumpness, all traces of freshness and grace have now completely disappeared. The thin mouth suggests anything but the blossoming of a smile. No longer is this a young woman rejoicing in her status, present or forthcoming, as mistress of a household. Rather, she gives the impression of a housewife aged by the fatigue and boredom of the never-ending round of daily chores.

Ill. 34

Saskia looks much older again in the drawings which show her in bed. There are several such works spread over the period 1635–40, and most of them portray not a sleeping but a sick woman. The cradle which is sometimes placed at the foot of her bed might suggest that this is Saskia after her confinements. But in other drawings the cradle is replaced by a nurse, who seems to have watched over her patient for a long time. Whether she is sewing, embroidering, or listening to Saskia, one has the impression that this woman's thoughts are not in the room. She has already heard Saskia complain too often, already come to her aid too many times. She has reached the stage of reconciling devotion and indifference, so familiar is she with the requirements of her patient and the signs of her illness.

As for Saskia, both her attitude and her expression vary. In one drawing she is leaning forward, her head resting on her arm, with an uneasy look on her bloated, faded face. In another, she is sitting up laboriously in bed and, although wrapped up in clothes and sheets, she puts her right hand to her breast, as if trying to protect herself from the cold—or as though she had just been shaken by one of those fits of coughing which rack consumptives. Elsewhere she is practically sitting upright in bed, quite still, sleeping or dozing perhaps, in any case completely given up to her exhausting illness. Yet another portrait shows her stretched out, very feeble, her head resting on a rather flat pillow, eyes open but blank, lips apart but incapable of uttering a word. One can guess how pale the face is, and how thin the body gnawed by fever. Rembrandt records all these gloomy, depressing aspects of long illnesses and exhausting watches with feeling, but without melodramatic pathos. It is easy to imagine him tip-toeing up to the canopy bed, and examining through the curtains the face of the

36 *The Charlatan.* 1635

37 *Pole carrying a Sabre and Baton.*
About 1632

38 *Study for a Beggar with Child.*
Between 1635 and 1640

woman whom he loved and who was growing weaker and weaker. Rembrandt must have made his drawings with a heavy heart, but his hand never lost its steadiness and adroitness.

Besides, these works quite clearly inform us about Rembrandt as well as Saskia. In particular, they reveal that, for him, all aspects of life are suitable material for the artist, even those which are distressing and painful. He did not even ignore subjects which it would have been good form to pass over in silence—certain etchings which he produced can be described as lewd. No doubt his aim was partly to shock people, to show a rather juvenile defiance of contemporary morality, but in all probability he was also motivated by a conviction that no part of life should be exempt from the artist's consideration— even physical love, even those human needs which are considered to be the lowest of all.

Rembrandt's paintings give only an incomplete idea of the great number of subjects which aroused his interest. His drawings include *Ill. 35* all manner of scenes: a snivelling child rebelling against his mother who has lifted him up, exposing the lower half of his abdomen; a baby wrapped in swaddling clothes, held in a woman's arms, and another baby which a woman has stood up by her side on still unsteady legs; older children wearing Christmas stars, or attracted by the pancake-woman and her sweet-smelling pan; two butchers carving up a pig; *Ill. 36* a quack at a fair delivering his patter to a group of gaping onlookers, a flute player with three men listening to him; Negroes going by, playing the trumpet . . .

In short, Rembrandt is not far removed from the genre painters in these works, and his selection of some of these themes may explain the admiration which he felt for Brouwer; although the latter's world with its drinking bouts and its brawls seems to have held no charms for him. He differs from the genre painters, however, in one main respect. They are fond of stressing the anecdotal, and often give the impression of addressing their public with the words: 'Look how odd these people are. You can count yourself lucky not to belong to such a rough-mannered section of the human race'. Rembrandt, on the contrary, depicts his various scenes without intending judgment to be passed on the characters involved: he wishes simply to portray things which exist in real life. His drawings utterly avoid the picturesque and show situations which are real, not contrived by the artist. He

74

simply looks upon them as reproductions of scenes he has witnessed, and it is owing to this realism that their impact on us is so direct.

It must be added that Rembrandt's drawings have more than a merely documentary value. They are also admirable in their purely artistic qualities. How eloquently he evokes Saskia confined to her bed! Where he depicts his sick, feeble wife, his line is slender, almost cautious. Elsewhere it is sweeping, impulsive and very firm. Gradations of wash also help to emphasize or soften shapes and to give the whole a most expressive unity.

Two works of this period, during which Rembrandt drew with authority and verve, are particularly worthy of note: *Young Woman at her Toilet* and *Study for the great Jewish Bride*. The fact that the *Ill. 39* attitudes in the first of these drawings are similar to those in a painting he executed in 1632, sometimes called *Bathsheba at her Toilet*, has given rise to the theory that the drawing preceded the picture, and in fact was a rough sketch for it. The two works are so divergent in style that this is hard to believe. Whereas the painting is minutely descriptive, the drawing suggests its subject with bold lines. The one is painstaking and analytical, the other impetuous and synthetical. Although the painting is by no means devoid of qualities, it does not possess the same supreme freedom as the drawing.

For many years, Rembrandt's drawings were plainly more advanced than his paintings, or even his etchings. The street scenes to be found in his etchings (his *Itinerant Musicians* for instance, and another which shows a pedlar selling rat-poison) are more elaborate than those in his drawings, but they also seem less audacious and less striking. Likewise, if one takes his *Great Jewish Bride* of 1635, the etched version is executed with far less freedom than the drawing.

In the etching, Rembrandt confines himself to description. He does *Ill. 40* his best to create an impression of lightness and thickness in the fabrics, and also of the silkiness of the girl's abundant hair. Moreover, the object of his draughtsmanship is to establish a series of subtle contrasts between greys, blacks and whites. In the drawing, on the other hand, his line has an existence independent of the subject. It does not merely reconstitute external reality, it compels us to a recognition of its own reality, it has a meaning of its own. If, for a moment, the woman's head is ignored, this becomes immediately apparent, for what one then sees is less a person than an exercise in drawing,

39 *Young Woman at her Toilet.* About 1635

40 *Study for the Great Jewish Bride.* About 1635

almost a scrawl: lines capering, winding, getting tangled up, bursting free, asserting in turn their power, zest and delicacy. This seething, passionate, even tender piece of draughtsmanship is unmistakably the expression of a man rebelling against conformity, affectation and lies, not for the sake of showing how little respect he has for conventional ideas but in order to proclaim unambiguously his own vision of truth.

A drawing like this gives a clear foretaste of the day when the same spirit would permeate all Rembrandt's work. With his energetic approach, such a passionate assertion of freedom was bound to lead to an ultimate liberation in all the fields of his artistic activity.

CHAPTER EIGHT

The temptation of baroque

Despite the fact that he was very much in demand as a portraitist in
Amsterdam during the 1630s, Rembrandt, not surprisingly, was not
satisfied merely with painting portraits. The desire to break away
from commonplace reality, already apparent in portraits of himself,
his wife, and the Jews, impelled him to go on producing other pictures
which gave scope to his imagination. In this respect, there is no difference between the work of his Leyden period and his output at this
time. He even reverted to a theme which he had already treated
on more than one occasion, that of the character reading or meditating in a room. His treatment of *St Paul in Prison* (1627) has al-   *Ill. 11*
ready been commented upon—there the saint's room had hardly any
life of its own.

Neither indeed has the room of the *St Paul* which he painted
around 1630, a work less anecdotal and more expressively lit. In his
St Anastasius (1631), however, the interior is of greater importance
than the subject. The saint's position at the back of the picture makes
him appear even smaller in relation to the architecture. One is immediately conscious of the great empty space which surrounds him in

the high, vaulted room. This space is encased by a shadow and permeated by a light which is first bright but then quickly becomes subdued. There is as much atmosphere of self-communion in this light as in the attitude of the patriarch with his large book.

The small-scale painting of a philosopher meditating, dated 1633, shows the same intention, except that here the architectural elements are different: the space is articulated above all by a spiral staircase, each step of which traps the light differently. This staircase also plays a role in the picture's theme, evoking the sinuous thoughts of the philosopher, developed in the shadowy extremities. Thus everything in this picture has more significance than in the preceding works. Even the woman stirring the fire in the right foreground is less surprising, after reflection, than she appears at first glance. Without doubt her function is to justify a second source of light, in contrast to the artificial daylight which shines through the window. But she also provides a contrast between everyday reality, utilitarian gestures, manual work, and the inactive meditation of the philosopher. Rembrandt was to paint other works in which he evoked the calm atmosphere of an interior, but this was the last he executed in his thirties, and at the same time the one in which he depicted gradations of light with the greatest finesse.

During the same period he painted subjects drawn from mythology: *Sophonisba receiving the poisoned Cup* (1634); *Minerva* (1635), who is probably none other than Saskia in pompous disguise; an *Andromeda* tied to a rock (c. 1632) which is rather reminiscent of the etchings of nudes in his Leyden period. He also painted *Diana bathing with Scenes from the Stories of Actaeon and Callisto* (1635), together with three 'rapes'—*Proserpine* (c. 1632), *Europa* (1632) and *Ganymede* (1635). In all these compositions expect the last the characters are small, their attitudes and their gestures attempt eloquence, but Rembrandt never gives the impression of being particularly enthralled by his subject. He may have been following the current trend for painting in the Italian style which was then being deprived of its leading disciples (Terbrugghen died in 1629, Jan Pynas in 1631, Lastman in 1633). Even so, odd details here and there indicate that he did not intend to adhere rigidly to this style of painting. Characters from Greek mythology are clearly transformed into ordinary Dutch men and women. Rembrandt does not even shrink from

41 *Christ in the Storm.* 1633

vulgarity, so much does he feel the need to bring the myth down to earth and give it an everyday setting.

Ill. 42 He was guided by the same purpose when he painted *Danaë* (1636), and this time the outcome was quite remarkable. One only has to compare this work with the Titian painting of the same subject in the Prado to realize the extent of Rembrandt's originality. So well-proportioned and so perfect is the splendid nude in Titian's painting that she can only belong to the world of fable. Sensuality is certainly an essential aspect of the picture, but it is a distant, sublimated, 'intellectual' sensuality. In Rembrandt's *Danaë*, nothing comes between the spectator and the woman stretched out on her bed. Nothing makes her inaccessible, nor is her position the passive one of Titian's nude. The sheet on the bed is pushed back and she turns towards an unseen visitor, beckoning him to come and discover her nakedness. Her bare body is made all the more alluring by its lack of anonymity. Rembrandt no longer resorts to the ugliness which he displayed in his etchings in order to lend character to his subject. He regards the body not as a collection of abstract shapes or an intellectual construction, but simply as a product of life, and for this reason he gives the body as much individuality as the face. It may be that this woman was herself dear to him or that she merely recalled the ecstatic sensations he had experienced when caressing Saskia's body. At any rate, the sight of this nude clearly did not leave him unmoved—the painting is the work of a lover of the female body, a man who combines sensuality with tenderness and respect.

Yet nudes in Rembrandt's work, or at least in his paintings, are a rarity. The explanation for this lies probably more in his puritanical environment than in his own inclinations. Every time his subject-matter allowed him to do so, Rembrandt showed with what attention, and even sometimes emotion, he observed the female body. In *Danaë* the theme of the nude is provided by mythology, in other works by the Bible. Pharaoh's daughter finding Moses, Susannah and the two elders, Bathsheba—all these subjects tempted him to paint nudes. The first of these works dates from about 1635, and the others from around 1632. He was to revert to these last two themes later on, for the Bible continued to be the main source of material for all his compositions.

Of the compositions which he executed shortly after setting up in

Amsterdam two were commissioned by the Prince Regent, Frederick Henry of Orange—*The Descent from the Cross* and *The Raising of the Cross*. It was Constantijn Huygens' intervention, and certainly his recommendation, which secured him these commissions. One may also assume that Huygens spoke to Rembrandt about the tastes of the client he had to satisfy. The Prince Regent liked baroque painters, and for his secretary, as we have already seen, there was no greater painter north of the Alps than Rubens. Understandably, therefore, Rembrandt wished to show that he was conversant with Rubens' interpretations of these two themes, which he must have been able to study in etchings. At the same time, he was also anxious to emphasize how different he was from the Antwerp painter.

Unlike his predecessor, Rembrandt does not lay stress in *The Raising of the Cross* on the physical effort made by the men erecting it, or the suffering which their jolting inflicts on the crucified figure. Rembrandt's aim is to highlight Christ nailed to the cross, as well as the perturbation which he himself feels at the thought that he has a share in the guilt of this martyrdom, that he is one of the actors in this drama. Indeed, the face of one of the men raising the cross is the painter's own. *Ill. 45*

Yet why did he think it necessary to dress up this character in fine clothes, including that handsome blue beret which he wears on his head? Of course, Rembrandt flaunts his elegance in his self-portraits, but it comes as something of a surprise that he should want to do the same in this painting, where the subject is so serious and the treatment is not lacking in gravity. An explanation for this seemingly odd behaviour is provided by a preparatory drawing. In this sketch, *Ill. 44*
Rembrandt is not only without a beret, but also rather carelessly dressed. Only in the painting, then, is he well-dressed. From this it is probably correct to conclude that only *for* the painting is he well-dressed, for reasons to do with the composition of the picture. As a painter, Rembrandt judged that he needed a few patches of blue in the centre of his picture to offset the otherwise subdued, dark colouring. Rembrandt had to vindicate the inclusion of these blue patches, and the objects with which he chose to do this were a beret and a doublet. In other words, Rembrandt here demonstrates that, far from being concerned exclusively with the expression of feelings and the logic of the narrative, he never loses sight of the fact that he also has

42 *Danaë*. 1636

purely pictorial problems, which are so important to him that he does
not hesitate, if need be, to sacrifice verisimilitude in order to obtain
a solution.

Rembrandt also participates in the action in *The Descent from the
Cross*—he is receiving the stiff body of Christ which the others are
lowering. This time he is bare-headed, and the expression on his face
is full of compassion. The blue now appears in the clothing of the

43 *Susanna bathing*. About 1637

character standing on the ladder, who is far from being well-dressed. The blue tints here are hardly more numerous than in the other painting. The overall colouring is not so much restrained as ascetic—sad, pale colours standing out against a nocturnal background. In this respect, Rembrandt differs completely from Rubens, who never dreamed of using such a muted palette. There are other points of divergence between the two painters. Rembrandt's draughtsmanship is less supple and his composition less animated; above all, the pathos in his picture is more austere than in Rubens'.

Many paintings which Rembrandt produced around the middle of the 1630s, however, do not show the same lack of movement. In *Abraham's Sacrifice* (1635), *The Blinding of Samson* (1636) or *The Angel leaving Tobit and his Family* (1637), he introduces the sharp, unexpected, terrifying movements of flight and assault. Tobit's family is no less disconcerted by the angel's sudden departure than Abraham by his sudden arrival.

Ill. 46   *The Blinding of Samson* contains violence of an extremely brutal kind. Rembrandt had already been attracted by the same subject in 1628 but in that painting he had depicted only the moment preceding the blinding—Samson asleep in Delilah's arms, with two armed men behind her preparing to fall upon him. Although we can thus imagine the scene which is about to take place, we are not obliged to witness it. In the 1636 painting, however, the onlooker is spared nothing. Samson has been thrown to the ground and lies struggling with the soldiers. One of them is lying under him, but has his arm round Samson's chest, holding him down. Another is slipping a chain onto his right wrist, a third threatening him with a spear and a fourth putting his eyes out with a dagger. Delilah can be seen fleeing with Samson's hair in her hand, while through the opening in the tent a light bursts in, striking Samson as implacably and as blindingly as the soldiers.

The savagery of this scene exceeds that in Caravaggio's *Martyrdom of St Matthew*. There is no shortage of cruelty in Caravaggio's painting, but it is depicted less forcefully and less blatantly than in *Samson*. Besides, this painting is also an exception in Rembrandt's work, so that one wonders whether he did not overdo things slightly in order to please Constantijn Huygens, who had a taste for horrific subjects. Rembrandt in fact presented Huygens with a picture by way of thanking him for securing the Prince Regent's commission, and the

44 *The Raising of the Cross.* 1633

dimensions which the painter mentions it as having tally exactly with those of *The Blinding of Samson.*

We know about this gift because the artist mentioned it in one of the seven letters which he wrote to the Prince Regent's secretary between 1636 and 1639. Another fact which these letters reveals is

45 *Raising of the Cross.* About 1633

that Rembrandt was commissioned by Huygens to paint three more compositions on the theme of Christ's life—*The Ascension, The Entombment* and *The Resurrection*. The correspondence also discloses when these works were completed, and the size of the fee the painter expected to receive for them. In the fourth letter of the series, dated 14 January 1639, Rembrandt expressed the hope that, for the last two of these pictures, 'Your Highness will not pay less than 1000 guilders per painting'. However, His Highness was not prepared to pay more than for the other works, that is, 600 guilders a canvas, and Rembrandt was obliged to declare himself satisfied with this sum—on condition, he added, that he receive a further 44 guilders for the ebony frames and the case.

It would clearly be of the greatest interest if the correspondence also made some mention of Rembrandt's artistic conceptions, but unfortunately it remains silent on this point. He was not an artist given to aesthetic analysis; he merely felt the need to explain why, having completed his *Ascension* in 1636, he should not have finished the other two works until 1639. The explanation he gave is that he wanted these paintings to have '*die meeste ende die naetuereelste beweechgelickheyt*'. The meaning of these words is debated even by specialists in old Dutch. Most writers take Rembrandt's words to mean that he had sought 'the greatest and most natural *movement*'. H. E. van Gelder, on the other hand, is of the opinion that *beweechgelickheyt* should be translated as *emotion* as, according to him, this is the way in which the word would have been construed in the 16th and 17th centuries. In fact, this dispute is really something of a sophistry, as we have the works which allow us to know not only what the artist intended but what he actually did.

In *The Ascension,* movement is undeniably the dominant facto.. Rembrandt seems to have based his painting on *The Assumption* by Titian which hangs in the Frari church, Venice. The attitude of Rembrandt's Christ recalls Titian's Virgin and, like the Venetian master, he also places an apostle in the foreground with his back to the onlooker and his arms open wide. Apart from this he immerses his scene in a chiaroscuro which clearly owes nothing to Titian's example.

Chiaroscuro also determines the appearance of the other two paintings. In *The Resurrection* the light is bright and mysterious. It almost gives the impression of exploding behind the angel lifting up the tombstone. The angel himself is completely bathed in light, and its dazzling, shattering appearance from the tomb has bowled over the soldiers much as an explosion might have done.

Ill. 47   In contrast to the sharpness of these movements, *The Entombment* is sorrowful and still. Here the gestures are restrained and, far from being theatrical, the light quietly underlines the grievous silence embodied in the attitudes and expressions of the characters. This is the most sensitive painting of the series, and the one most laden with inner life. If it was this picture which Rembrandt had in mind when

46 *The Blinding of Samson.* 1636

47 *The Entombment.* 1639

48 *The Death of the Virgin.* 1639

he recorded his wish to express much '*beweechgelickheyt*', the term may then be translated as emotion; if, on the other hand, he is held to have been referring to *The Resurrection*, then the correct translation must be movement.

Baroque tendencies are again in evidence in other works of the same period. They are apparent in *Christ before Pilate*, a scene which Rembrandt depicted both in painting (1633) and in etching (1635—36), and staged with a great number of characters, who are so crammed together that the composition loses almost all clarity. They are also displayed in prints such as *The Angel appearing to the Shepherds* (1634) and *The Death of the Virgin* (1639), two etchings which in all other respects are highly dissimilar. The first work is dominated by darkness, while harsh or more subdued gleams of light twist and flicker against the gloomy background. In the second work it is the light which dominates, and there are a few straight lines to contrast with the abundance of curves. Further, although there are still traces of a descriptive style, notably in the clothes and the furniture, at many points Rembrandt's line is merely allusive. This work is a forerunner of the etchings which Rembrandt was to produce some ten years later, when his art was as free as it was masterly.

Ill. 48

CHAPTER NINE

Homage to classicism

The fervour with which Rembrandt embraced baroque around 1636 did not last for very long. Only three years later his style had become much quieter, and if he never fully abandoned movement in his paintings, it was henceforth more infrequently used and less violent.

The influence which prompted Rembrandt to adopt this calmer approach, to move away from the art of Caravaggio and similar painters, was Italian painting of the 15th and 16th centuries. This is surprising but true. Rembrandt, who had never been to Italy, who had even rejected the idea of going there when Constantijn Huygens had recommended him to do so, was in fact by no means ignorant or disdainful of the art of the classical and preclassical periods: he paid close attention to it, consulted it and followed its example. It will be recalled that the explanation Rembrandt gave Huygens for his refusal to go and examine the works of Raphael and Michelangelo in Florence or Rome was that Renaissance painting could just as well be studied in the Netherlands. There were indeed many works by Italian artists in Holland at that time. As Sir Kenneth Clark remarks in his

50 *The Last Supper, after Leonardo de Vinci.* About 1635

Rembrandt and the Italian Renaissance, 'In 1630 Amsterdam was the centre of the art trade of the world. Collections were sent there to be sold from all over Europe, in particular from Italy.'

More specifically, the same author states that in the 1640s the Andrea Vendramin collection, which comprised over 100 pictures by Venetian artists (Bellini, Giorgione, Titian, Tintoretto, etc.) was put up for sale in Amsterdam by Gerrit van Uylenburgh, Saskia's cousin. Van Uylenburgh's house contained a studio, where he had copies made of all the works which passed through his hands. Rembrandt was thus in a good position to familiarize himself with them, and we can be sure that he availed himself of the opportunity to do so.

More than that, Rembrandt bought Italian paintings himself. The inventory of his possessions drawn up in 1656 includes a picture by Palma Vecchio, a *Head* and a *Virgin* by Raphael, and Giorgione's

Christ and the Samaritan Woman. Even if some of these attributions were held to be dubious or incorrect, the important thing is that Rembrandt wished to possess such works. As he could not acquire all the originals which he would doubtless have liked, he bought instead etchings after these originals. The inventory is quite clear on this point: Rembrandt's house contained series of prints after Raphael, Michelangelo, Titian and others, and beyond doubt he studied and made use of them. We have already seen how his *Ascension* recalls Titian's *Assumption.* Numerous other examples are quoted by Sir Kenneth Clark. The close similarities which Sir Kenneth establishes between works by Italian painters and works by Rembrandt himself may not always be equally convincing. Rembrandt could have found some of his attitudes simply by looking around him or imagining them, without necessarily always taking them from other artists. All in all, however, the thesis is most revealing.

We have in our possession copies of Italian etchings and drawings which were made in Rembrandt's studio. While some of these have been attributed to his pupils, others are incontestably his own work. Among the first category it is surprising to find drawings after Gentile Bellini and Carpaccio, but, even more surprisingly, the second category includes a *Calumny of Apelles* and an *Entombment,* the original inspiration for which were two etchings by Mantegna. That Rembrandt should have thought of copying an artist so enamoured of hard, clear-cut shapes is evidence of a willingness to study styles totally opposed to his own in order to enrich his art.

Rembrandt also copied a print which reproduced *The Last Supper* *Ill. 50* by Leonardo da Vinci. This was a work which so preoccupied him that he returned to the theme on several other occasions. He was first attracted to it at the height of his baroque period, around the middle of the 1630s, so his version was not a slavish imitation of the Italian master's work. Firstly, he rejected the strict perspective which da Vinci imparts to his precisely constructed room. In order to place the characters and the table nearer to the wall in the background he dispensed with the vanishing-lines, and so deprived the room of its depth. Second, he replaced the window behind Christ by a canopy, thus substituting irregular folds of soft material for regular architectural features. Furthermore, whereas Leonardo's Christ occupies the centre of the picture so that the point where the vanishing-lines join is in his

97

51 *Self-portrait.* 1640

52 *Saskia with a red Flower.* 1641

face, in Rembrandt's version he has been pushed back slightly towards the left, and the canopy is not aligned symmetrically behind him. The two groups of apostles on either side of Christ are also a little asymmetrical. Clearly, then, Rembrandt was reluctant to submit entirely to da Vinci's influence. He would not—perhaps, more correctly, he could not—completely restrain his own natural instincts, which fundamentally were not those of a classical artist. This is even more clearly demonstrated in another drawing based on the same subject, in which he allows himself a greater freedom of interpretation than in the first version.

Ill. 49   Further confirmation is provided by his painting *Samson's Wedding* (1638), in which he, like Leonardo, depicts people gathered round a table for a meal. Delilah's triangular shape and the blank spaces which cut her off from the rest of the characters bear an obvious resemblance to Leonardo's painting, but the asymmetry in this work is more pronounced than in Rembrandt's copy of *The Last Supper,* and the movements are less ordered. None the less, Rembrandt was haunted by classicism and never ceased to flirt with it in his work.

    Two paintings which appeared on the Amsterdam art market in 1639 made a particular impression on him—Raphael's *Baldassare Castiglione* and Titian's so-called *Portrait of Ariosto.* The Raphael painting came up for sale at a public auction, and the proof that

Ill. 53   Rembrandt saw it is that he has left us a rough sketch of it. He probably executed this sketch while the auction was actually in progress, since it is quickly drawn, and is also marked with the price which the picture fetched—3500 guilders. Rembrandt may well have wanted to acquire this portrait for his own collection, and must have recorded with regret the final figure, which was doubtless too high for him to contemplate.

    Not only was this rough sketch executed at speed, it was also not a very close likeness of the picture it was meant to evoke. Baldassare Castiglione was the Renaissance diplomat and author of *The Courtier,* and Raphael's picture brought out his distinguished appearance and his aristocratic reserve. In Rembrandt's sketch, however, he has the look of an overbearing, rather savage conqueror. Yet beyond a doubt Rembrandt had studied the portrait closely, had absorbed it in his memory, and was later to deploy his knowledge of it. He was also to make use of Titian's work. Only a short while after seeing these pictures he

53 *Baldassare Castiglione, after Raphael.* 1639

produced two new self-portraits which differed from the ones which
had gone before.

The first of these was an etching (1639) and the second a painting
(1640). In the etching the face is portrayed at the same angle as *Ill. 54*
Baldassare Castiglione's, while the position of the left arm and the
fullness of the sleeve are features borrowed from Titian. Nevertheless,
the resulting work is neither hybrid nor eclectic but original, and in
it Rembrandt asserts his personality in the expressiveness as much as
in the style. His lines are less flowing than those of Titian and Raphael, his folds are more twisted, and the play of light and shade in
his work is more complex and less serene. Moreover, the face is tense,
the forehead creased, and the gaze betokens impatience. There is
something disrespectful and nonconformist about the slanting angle
of the beret which has nothing in common with either *Baldassare
Castiglione* or the so-called *Ariosto*. In this print, then, Rembrandt
followed the balanced example of classical art, but was not yet ready
to curb his own temperament entirely.

54 *Self-portrait.* 1639

Ill. 51   In the *Self-portrait* which he painted in the following year, on the other hand, his rebellious nature is submissive. His gaze remains steady, but is no longer piercing. There is now no trace of affectation in the way he wears the dark brown robe with its fur collar, and the broad velvet beret, whose gentle curves flow in a horizontal direction. No more is he an art student in disguise or a soldier of arrogant appearance, but a real man of distinction, full of calm assurance and becoming dignity. As a painting, this portrait is also highly distinguished and self-assured. In the National Gallery, London, where one may compare the work with the so-called *Ariosto*, one is easily convinced that Rembrandt is inferior to Titian neither in the refinement of his tints nor in his evocation of textures. He could hardly have absorbed the lessons of his Italian models better.

Of course, Rembrandt had not assimilated classical influences once and for all. The classicism of this portrait represents more of an aspiration than a genuinely durable state of affairs, and baroque touches were later to reappear in his work. It would not have been natural for Rembrandt to have undergone a radical conversion. He was not the sort of artist who had only to admire someone else's painting in order utterly to repudiate his past and his most profound inclinations. He was not, therefore, to become an out-and-out classical painter, but he did moderate his taste for baroque and, above all, he did seek a greater clarity of composition.

Some other portraits which he executed between 1639 and 1641 illustrate this evolution—*Portrait of a fashionable young Lady* (1639), *Young Lady with a Fan standing at a Window* (1641), which ranks among the masterpieces of this period, *Young Girl at a Window* (1641) and *Saskia with a red Flower* (1641). His *Fashionable young Lady* of 1639 is a three-quarters portrait, but all the others are full-face, and the attitudes of the models instantly reveal the geometrical nature of the arrangement. In all these portraits a relationship between curves and straight lines can be distinguished, as can the sharp contrast between the oval shape of the model's head and the triangle formed by her body. In addition to this clarity of arrangement there is a new calmness in draughtsmanship and expression. These faces seem to have more individual character than in the portraits of previous years, and the somewhat idealized style has made their features more regular and more attractive.

Ill. 52

55 Elephant. 1637

CHAPTER TEN

Landscapes and animal subjects

Although the human being was to remain the main subject of Rembrandt's work, this did not prevent him from producing paintings and drawings of animals at the same time. They are usually to be found in his compositions: Balaam's ass, or the ass in *Flight into Egypt;* Tobit's dog, or the eagle in *The Rape of Ganymede;* the horse of the good Samaritan or the horse which gallops along with Pluto's chariot in *The Rape of Proserpine.* Sometimes a cat or a dog appears in an unexpected context, for example in the *Parable of the Labourers in the Vineyard* (1637), and they help to give the scene a more realistic and familiar flavour.

In 1635 and 1639, Rembrandt painted four canvases featuring peacocks, bitterns, and other birds. All of them are dead, and in three cases it is clearly indicated that the birds are shot game. On one occasion the hunter is also portrayed—he can be seen holding a bittern in his hand and his face is Rembrandt's own. This is not *Ill. 60* merely an instance of Rembrandt showing off in a different costume, for here it is not he who occupies the most prominent position. He stands at the back of the picture in semi-darkness, while the scene is dominated by the bird, or rather its plumage, which is mottled with sparkling light and pockets of shadow. Once again, Rembrandt here gives evidence of his mastery in rendering textures. It almost seems as if his sole reason for painting these birds was to make us aware of the subtle shimmering effect and to give us a well-defined and varied range of tactile sensations. The spectator has the impression of running not only his eyes but his fingers over the warm, light down of the birds, and their large, stiff, glossy feathers.

Ill. 55   His *Elephant* (1637), a drawing in black chalk, also imparts strong tactile sensations. His very free style does not prevent him from reproducing realistically all the animal's characteristic features, including the skin. Although Rembrandt turned only occasionally to

56 *A Lion Hunt.* 1641

57 *Study for a Bird of Paradise.* 1640

animal subjects, such a work proves admirably that he knew how to handle them more naturally and authoritatively than all but a very few 'professional' animal-painters.

The elephant was not the only exotic animal which aroused his interest. Using a pen, which he handles with both firmness and suppleness, he drew in particular a series of *Lions*. A few lines, a few spots of wash, and the beast is there before us, majestic and menacing, although lying on the ground. In Rembrandt's three etchings of *A Lion Hunt,* the biggest of which is dated 1641, the lion has naturally a quite different appearance. In each of these works, which were inspired by Rubens' example, the animal is ferocious, aggravated by the man fighting him. Now the scene is full of impulsive movements,

Ill. 56

107

58 *The Windmill.* 1641

slender lines, and bodies which have been reduced to flashing apparitions by the sharp tumult of the struggle.

The hunts are, of course, situated in landscapes, but these are barely indicated. In other Rembrandt works, too, the landscape generally fulfils the sole purpose of providing a backcloth for the scene taking place in the foreground, but every so often this background possesses a breadth and quality which only a true landscape-painter could produce. Rembrandt began to display this aspect of his art openly in 1636, in a series of paintings which rank among the finest landscapes ever produced by Dutch artists. These landscapes are few in number: during the whole of his career Rembrandt painted only about fifteen, over half of which date from before 1642.

It will be recalled that in Leyden Rembrandt had seen a landscape-painter at work who might have been expected to influence his approach—van Goyen. In fact, Rembrandt's landscapes, at least as far as the paintings are concerned, are nothing like van Goyen's. His affinities with Hercules Seghers, on the other hand, are very clear. Thus, at a time when Dutch painters were being led by their realistic tendencies to portray town and countryside as a devoted observer might discover them, Rembrandt remained faithful to the composite landscape which existed nowhere but in his own imagination. The essential function of Rembrandt's pictures is less to reproduce external

59 *The Omval near Amsterdam.* 1645

61 *Landscape with Stone Bridge.* About 1638

reality than to give material form to a vision which expresses a state
of mind. Thus, among the trees, streams and anchorages can be found
ruins, medieval churches, towns built on mountainsides, and even an
obelisk not far away from the paddle-wheel of a mill. The light
accentuates the eeriness of these sites, its uneasy tremor contrasting
with the threat of a storm or the menace of a deepening darkness.

When Rembrandt started to produce landscape etchings around
1640, this atmosphere of pathos vanished. The sky now becomes
empty of clouds, leaving only a huge, light surface in front of which
may stand out a rough cottage, or the great sails of a windmill facing   *Ill. 58*
the wind. On the whole, these works have a realistic look about them
which his painted landscapes do not possess. Yet however carefully
Rembrandt may draw the mill, for instance, with all its distinctive

◁ 60 *Self-portrait with Bittern.* 1639

62 *View of Amsterdam.* About 1640

63 *View of Windsor.* About 1640

features and mechanical apparatus, it does not remain a cold description. No doubt he still remembered his father's mill, which he must have explored with wonderment when he was a child. No doubt, too, he wished to make it as impressive as he remembered it. He therefore makes it loom up in the foreground, a massive, almost heroic shape, which dominates the poky little house behind it.

Realism is also the chief characteristic of his *View of Amsterdam*, *Ill. 62* another etching of around the same time. Before us lies the countryside, flat and soaked with water, while on the horizon one can see the silhouette of the city with its houses, windmills, church towers and masts. The diffused and slightly veiled light of Holland is no less finely observed than the tangible objects and everything is suggested by a line which has both sharpness and delicacy.

Rembrandt's *View of Windsor* (1640) diverges from this *View of* *Ill. 63* *Amsterdam* not only because, as a pen-and-ink drawing touched up with wash, it necessarily produces different effects to those of the etching, but also because it is not based on any direct contact with reality. There is no proof that Rembrandt ever went to England, so that his acquaintance with this scene can only have come through other pictures. His natural inclination was to interpret these in his own way, and he put his own stamp on the scene by projecting on it his special kind of light. The work he thus produced has the look not of a copy, but of an original creation, as natural and spontaneous as drawings inspired by a direct visual contact with the outside world.

64 *Rembrandt's house in Amsterdam*

65 *Rembrandt's Press*

CHAPTER ELEVEN

The end of an era

For the first few years of their marriage, Rembrandt and Saskia went on living in van Uylenburgh's house. They moved out around 1636 and settled first in the Nieuwe Doelenstraat, and later in the Zwanenburgerstraat, not far away from there. In 1639 they decided to return to the Breestraat, where they bought a spacious house, the one now known as 'Rembrandt's house'. (In fact, the house is no longer quite the same as when Rembrandt lived there. Nowadays it also comprises a second storey surmounted by a cornice with a classical pediment, whereas then the only thing above the first floor was a stepped gable.) The selling price of the house was 13,000 guilders: of this the artist undertook to pay 1200 guilders on the day when the property was handed over to him, that is 1 May 1639, a further 1200 guilders six months later, 850 guilders on 1 May 1640, and the remainder during the course of the next five or six years.

Although the purchase of this house indicates that Rembrandt considered himself (and was considered by others) to be a man who could allow himself an important outlay, the fact that he was granted these delays in payment also reveals that his resources were insufficient for him to settle up at once. In point of fact, he admitted his need for revenue when writing to Constantijn Huygens about pictures painted for the Prince Regent. Between 12 January and 17 February 1639, he sent him no less than five letters on this subject, in the last of which he insisted that he should 'finally receive his 1244 guilders', which he judged to be 'well-deserved'. One ought not to conclude that without this money, which the Prince Regent ordered to be remitted to Rembrandt on 17 February, the artist would have been unable to pay off the first portion of his debt. It should simply be remembered that this debt existed, and that Rembrandt was to have considerable difficulty in meeting his obligations—particularly as he was not prepared to sacrifice everything else in order to own this house. He retained his passion for collecting, which he had no intention of repressing.

For the time being, however, there was no cause for alarm. Saskia was still well-off, and Rembrandt's good name as an artist was unsullied. He continued to obtain commissions, and to receive pupils for instruction. Each such pupil paid him 100 guilders a year, plus a percentage of the money fetched by sales of his work. One of his pupils, Philips Koninck, was to make a name for himself as a landscape-painter. Before him, Rembrandt had taught Ferdinand Bol and Govert Flinck, who were also to earn a place in the history of Dutch painting. Rembrandt must have been a good teacher, for up to about 1660 large numbers of young men wished to study under his guidance. During this period he had more than thirty pupils and some of these were to become, if not great painters, at any rate no mean artists.

The regard in which Rembrandt was held is illustrated by the fact that, on publishing the second edition in 1641 of *Description of the Town of Leyden*, Johannes Orlers, a former mayor of the town, judged it necessary to supplement the text by a passage on Rembrandt. The mayor writes with evident pride of his former fellow-citizen who, during his attachment to van Swanenburgh, 'progressed so much that art-lovers were astonished and it was obvious that with time he would become an excellent painter'. He was then sent to study with 'the very celebrated Pieter Lastman', with whom he stayed for about six months, before he 'decided to practise painting on his own and in complete independence, and so felicitous was his style that he became one of the most famous painters of our century. As his art much appealed to the people of Amsterdam, and they often com-

66 David taking leave of Jonathan. 1642

missioned him to do portraits and other paintings, he decided to leave Leyden and go to Amsterdam . . . where he is still living in 1641.'

In the same year that this text appeared, Rembrandt sketched out a work which also tells us about his relationship with his environment. This was an allegorical composition whose aim was to celebrate *The Concord of the State*. Its main components come as a surprise: armed men on horseback about to leave for the fray; a chained lion which looks as though it is eager to leap up, with a bundle of arrows under its paw, symbolizing concord; the coats of arms of various Dutch towns; the inscription *Soli Deo gloria,* and a representation of Justice in prayer. The treatment, that of a sketch executed with virtually a single tint, is quite lively, but the general effect is not very convincing. Obviously, such a subject, such a 'reality' even, was alien to Rembrandt. The interesting thing about the picture is that he must have been commissioned to handle this theme, for he would certainly never have dreamed of doing so otherwise. This shows two things about Rembrandt's relations with his clientele—that he was popular and that he was also misjudged.

Rembrandt's success as a portraitist and the will with which he applied himself to satisfying his sitters' requirements doubtless led people to believe that the painter shared the outlook and general feelings of his society. Although he treated his clients with respect when executing a portrait, as soon as he painted a composition his imagination came into play and the refractory side of his originality emerged. If he found the subject pleasing, the result was a work in which he unfolded all his genius. If, on the other hand, the subject left him indifferent, he felt fettered, as is the case in this work. It should not, therefore, be surprising that this composition never went beyond the rough sketch stage. The question of whether it was turned down by those who had commissioned it or rejected by the man who was to paint it is of no significance. Its importance is that it enables us to see how, even at that time, relations between Rembrandt and his fellow-citizens were less harmonious than one would suppose from his portraits. The respect which he was shown was thus in part based on a misunderstanding, of which the painter was quite possibly hardly more aware than his public.

However that may be, respect for Rembrandt was not merely confined to the Netherlands. Two of his paintings figured in the collection of Charles I of England as early as the 1630s, and when, in 1640, the Englishman Peter Mundy noted down what he had seen in Amsterdam in his journal, he mentioned just one name in connection with painting—'Rimbrantt'. In France, too, the painter Claude Vignon wrote in November 1641 (in Italian) to Francois Langlois, called Ciartres, a dealer in paintings and publisher of prints: 'When you go to Amsterdam give Rembrandt my regards, and bring back something by him. Tell him also that yesterday I valued the *Prophet Balaam*, which Mr. Lopez bought from him and which will be sold in December along with other works'—which were to include Titian's so-called *Ariosto*. (Lopez was a man who combined the functions of art dealer and agent to the King of France, for whom he bought supplies and victuals in Holland. It was also he who purchased the painting *Baldassare Castiglione* in Amsterdam in 1639.)

If Rembrandt had weighed up his position at this moment in his life, he would have had every reason to be pleased with his standing as a painter. His family life did not give similar cause for satisfaction, for in 1640 he suffered two bereavements. He lost his third child, Cornelia, who had only just been christened, and also his mother. From a document dated 2 November 1640 it emerges that his mother's heirs (his father had already been dead for ten years) had been reduced to four: Rembrandt, his brothers Adriaen and Willem, and his sister Elizabeth.

A short while later, Saskia was preparing herself for yet another confinement, and on 22 September 1641, she gave birth to a son to whom they gave the name Titus. It is easy to imagine how anxious the parents must have felt about the precarious life of their fourth child. They must have wondered whether he would share the fate of all the rest, whether, with the baptism forms barely completed, they might not once more be thinking of the funeral. In fact, Titus was to survive, but his mother remained a sick woman. She grew weaker and weaker, and on 5 June 1642, the moment of death was judged to be imminent enough for a notary to be summoned to draw up a will. Saskia decided to bequeath all her belongings to Titus, and to such other children as she might still have, but for as long as he did not remarry, Rembrandt was to hold the entire legacy in usufruct. It would not be necessary for him to draw up an inventory, or for the inheritance to be declared to the Chamber of Orphans. Rembrandt,

Saskia was convinced, would discharge his duties conscientiously, and he was to be the guardian of their children and administer their estate.

That Saskia should have asked the notary to stipulate *children* is rather curious, as she had only one child and was never to give birth to another. Nine days later she was dead. She was buried on 19 June, and on 9 July Rembrandt bought her a tomb in the Oude Kerk (Old Church) in Amsterdam. The death of Saskia, at the age of thirty, marked for Rembrandt the end of an era.

Ill. 67 1642 was also an important year for him in the field of artistic creation. It was then that he completed the greatest composition that he had ever produced, and one of his boldest paintings, a work which was to become famous under the name of *The Night Watch*. It is now common knowledge that this title does not represent the artist's intentions and does not tally with the picture in its original state. It only acquired its nocturnal appearance later as a result of the darkening of the various layers of varnish with which the canvas was covered. The real subject is the parade of the Civic Guard under Captain Frans Banning Cocq, 'nobleman of Purmerlandt and Ilpendam'. In other words, this is another group portrait. However, there are considerable differences between Rembrandt's picture and the traditional group portrait of other Dutch artists.

Normally when companies of the Civic Guard were portrayed the same method was adopted as for an *Anatomy Lesson*—a juxtaposition of characters in more or less set attitudes. Even Frans Hals, for all his efforts to make grouping less rigid, to get his officials

67 The Night Watch. 1642

to make fairly natural gestures and look and almost talk to each other, for all the unconstraint which he showed, never failed to respect the fundamental requirement of his sitters—that everyone should be easily visible and that no one face should be neglected or disregarded in relation to the others. In 1639 Hals was commissioned to execute another group portrait—*The Officers of the Militia Company of St. George*. His subjects are lined up in two rows, one above the other, so that they look as though they are standing on the steps of a staircase. Although not all of them direct their gaze to the front, and some faces are turned slightly to the right or left, we are nevertheless given the impression that the characters are posing, and that each individual is concerned with appearing to the best advantage.

Rembrandt's models must have wanted him to do the same for them, but he had no desire to satisfy their wishes. Far from ranging them in two rows and giving them as little movement as possible, he paints them at the very moment when their marching orders have arrived and they present a spectacle of confused agitation. Whereas the captain and the lieutenant are already moving forward with determined strides, the reactions of their colleagues are quite different. While some of them hardly move at all, others are gesticulating, and almost all are looking or moving in opposite directions. Here spears are raised, there muskets are being loaded or examined, elsewhere a halberd is held impassively or a banner flaunted. The uniforms are also varied, cylindrical hats alternating with plumed ones, caps with richly burnished helmets. Figures which have nothing to do with the company serve to add to the confusion—in the left foreground, a boy running away; in the middle ground, a little girl who has strayed into the group; finally, on the right, a dog barking, frightened by the rolling of the drum.

It might be objected that Rembrandt overdoes the effect, that his eagerness to break away from stiff, conventional presentations and make each attitude a natural one leads him to include much that is gratuitous and arbitrary. Certainly, if the criterion of realism is applied to the picture, there are many details whose presence is difficult to justify. Yet in his work the visionary always tends to take precedence over the observer of facts, and it should not therefore be surprising that on this occasion, as on many others, he wished to interpret the scene in his own way. Besides, there can be no doubt that the painting is the better for it, for a realistic portrayal of these bourgeois in soldier's uniform would have led, not necessarily to a commonplace picture, as Hals had proved, but to one lacking in mystery, poetry, and all qualities other than those of fine brushwork. Instead, ordinary reality is left behind. These characters are stripped of their ordinariness and step, transformed, into the realm of legend.

The reason for this transformation is the light. It looks like the warm light of a late afternoon, but its real source is Rembrandt himself—he directs it without always taking physical laws into account. He uses it not only to bring out certain characters but also to link up the various parts of the picture, and to give it balance and an instantly captivating lyricism.

Against a background of greenish or brownish grey, light blues, olive greens, golden browns, blacks and reds, either stand out sharply or merge gently into the rest. And what could be richer, nobler, more subtle or more marvellous than the yellow uniform of the lieutenant, which provides a solemn contrast with the black costume, striped with a red sash, which is worn by the captain?

The necessity of balancing and illuminating the colours may not determine all the attitudes, but it does explain the positioning of certain characters, and even the presence of the most unwonted of them—the little girl in the light dress. At the point where she appears Rembrandt needed a light patch of colour which would be bright but not too large, for without her the lightness of the lieutenant's uniform would be too isolated, and would tie up badly with the rest of the picture. The light patch introduced by the little girl prevents this uniform from being too obtrusive and at the same time illuminates a part of the composition which might have contained a mere pocket of shade. It must never be forgotten that Rembrandt is something more than a mere storyteller, and, if all his clients asked him to do was to document their activities, he never forgot that, as a painter, he also had pictorial problems to solve. He had already demonstrated this by giving himself a blue beret for *The Raising of the Cross,* and he also showed it here by introducing against all likelihood, almost against all reason, this strange, brilliant figure of the little girl with a *Ill. 68* cock tied to her waistband, whose features vaguely resemble Saskia's.

Other recurring concerns of the painter appear in *The Night Watch*—notably in the interplay of the lines drawn by the spears, and

in the parallel line established between the staff of the banner and the musket of the guard dressed in red standing beneath it. Even the dog has more than anecdotal value, for although it represents one of those commonplace features which Rembrandt liked to bring into play in order to increase verisimilitude, it is also a means, in this case, of animating and filling out the composition. Like the little girl, it gives a certain emphasis to a weak point in the painting, fills up a gap, and provides justification for the curves and tints which link the lieutenant to the drum.

A painting whose logic is of a pictorial kind rarely meets with approval as readily as one with a plausible narrative. How, then, was the picture received by the artist's contemporaries and, in particular, by the men who had commissioned it? It always used to be held that the Civic Guard was taken aback and disappointed by *The Night Watch* and that it even provoked an estrangement between public and painter. Nowadays, this opinion is contradicted by certain historians, who cite as their main piece of evidence that the picture was after all hung in the Great Hall of the Civic Guards *(Kloveniers-doelen)* for which it was commissioned. Yet the fact that it was accepted does not necessarily prove that it pleased everyone. It would have been sufficient for the painting to please the captain, and for him to have been a man of influence, to secure it the position which it was destined to receive. Significantly, the captain was the very man who had no cause for complaint. There he stands in the foreground, his face fully visible, his rank instantly asserting itself. Despite his small stature (he may not have been taller than he appears in the painting) the lieutenant could also declare himself well satisfied with the result. His face appears only in profile, but it can be made out quite clearly, and the splendid uniform which he wears immediately attracts attention to him.

As far as the other characters are concerned, however, none (with the exception of the man attending to his musket on the left) is permitted to show more than a part of his body, and in certain cases even the face is not displayed in full. More than that, the way in which the light falls on their faces in so capricious that the features are blurred and the likeness weakened. Those treated in this manner can therefore be expected to have felt cheated, particularly as each member of the company paid roughly the same amount (100 guilders) and consequently felt entitled to be given as much weight as the next man. There can be no doubt then that some of the sitters were displeased with the result. This is not to say that Rembrandt completely lost the regard of his compatriots overnight. In 1642 his prestige was too high to be destroyed at one stroke by the creation of a single disturbing, revolutionary work.

Not surprisingly, therefore, Seymour Slive is able, in his book *Rembrandt and his Critics*, to quote remarks and verses written between 1645 and 1660 in which the artist is mentioned with admiration. After all, *The Night Watch* was not the only painting which he produced, and even those offended by this canvas must still have found remarkable others which he had executed. This indeed is the conclusion one reaches on reading the poems which Mr. Slive reproduces. Not one of them singles *The Night Watch* out for praise.

The very opposite is true, for there are works published in the 17th century—quoted again by Slive—which confirm that the painting aroused critical comment. These texts did not appear until after Rembrandt's death, but this does not necessarily mean that the opinions there expressed could not already have been encountered at an earlier date. When Samuel van Hoogstraten writes of *The Night Watch* in his *Inleyding tot de Hooge Schoole der Schilder-Konst anders de Zichtbaere Werelt* (1678), the very terms which he uses indicate that he is taking into account appraisals of the picture which were made shortly after its completion. Having studied under Rembrandt in the early 1640s, van Hoogstraten was in a particularly good position to know these reactions. 'Many people were of the opinion', he remarks, 'that, instead of presenting a series of individual portraits which he had been commissioned to do, the artist took his own wishes too much into consideration. Nevertheless, whatever shortcomings this work may be reproached with, it will outlive all its competitors. It is so striking in pictorial conception, so animated in movement and so powerful that, in the estimation of some, all the other canvases which hang beside it in the hall of the Civic Guard are made to look like playing cards.' Phraseology like this leaves no room for doubt about the impression which *The Night Watch* produced. If the picture was admired by some (although not unreservedly so, as even Hoogstraten adds that he would have liked it to contain more light), many people were bluntly critical of it.

Nothing in *Cominciamento e progresso dell'arte dell'intagliare in rame, colle vite di molti de' più eccellenti Maestri delle stessa Professione* (1686), a work by the Italian author, Filippo Baldinucci, serves to shake this conclusion. Baldinucci in fact related what he had been told by the Danish painter Bernhardt Keil, who was also a pupil of Rembrandt's in the early 1640s. Although he remarks that *The Night Watch* brought Rembrandt a fame which few other Dutch painters had known, he explains this phenomenon principally by the fact that a halberd is put into perspective so convincingly that one has the impression of seeing it in its entire length, whereas in actual fact it is shorter than half an arm. For the rest, Baldinucci finds that the composition is so confused that it is hardly possible to distinguish one character from another.

Nor is this all. Usually, when an innovatory painting excites favourable comment, it influences and is imitated by other artists. *The Night Watch,* however, remained a completely isolated work. It burst into Dutch painting completely unheralded, and once it had been created no one felt tempted to follow its example. At least, no one gave in to such a temptation even if they felt it. The group portrait in the Netherlands remained, after *The Night Watch,* exactly the same as it had been before. Everything proceeded as though this revolutionary work had never seen the light of day. This is surely conclusive proof that *The Night Watch* was ignored and its formula rejected.

That Hoogstraten and a few others should have regarded it with admiration makes no difference to this cardinal fact. Similarly, one is not entitled to deduce that the picture was really popular simply because Gerrit Lundens copied it. What one may conclude from this copy is that at the time *The Night Watch* left Rembrandt's studio it was not in every respect identical to the painting we know today. After the artist's death a scroll was added to the background near the arch, bearing the names of those who had clubbed together to have their portraits painted: they apparently thought that they could not be identified and wished their presence to be attested, at the very least, by the inscription of their names. Apart from that, when the canvas was removed to the Town Hall in Amsterdam in 1715 and was found to be too large to hang in the position it was intended to occupy, it was forthwith reduced in size—about 20 centimetres were taken off the top and the bottom, about ten off the right-hand side, and over 60 off the left-hand side. In other words, it was far from being considered a venerable masterpiece. This reduction also altered the composition of the picture—the scale was diminished and the rhythm and clarity of the arrangement disturbed.

There is one other fact which proves with what little enthusiasm *The Night Watch* was received by most contemporaries. Only twice more during the remaining 27 years of his life was Rembrandt asked to paint a group portrait—in 1656 and 1662. The public preferred Bartholomeus van der Helst, an able portraitist who respected his subjects to the point of boredom, and with whom, consequently, clients could be quite sure of taking no risks.

The fact that he was not commissioned to do a group portrait for another 14 years was probably a matter of no regret to Rembrandt, as his overriding concern was to express and satisfy himself. He was also concerned to bring out spiritual life, on which he set a high value and which commissioned pictures did not as a rule allow him to display. Although, therefore, *The Night Watch* and the death of Saskia marked the end of a chapter in his life and his artistic activity, it would be wrong to say that Rembrandt henceforth embarked on a completely fresh course. He simply turned a little further aside from a world to which he had only ever given part of his being, and the most superficial part at that.

He produced another painting in 1642, far smaller than *The Night Watch,* but nevertheless deserving of special attention—*David taking* *Ill. 66* *Leave of Jonathan.* Rembrandt may have been identifying himself and Saskia with the subject. At any rate, this is a work of great tenderness, and the face of Jonathan, to whom he imparts his own features, bears the expression of a man bracing himself to console another, while grief wells up in his own heart. The work is no less delicate from the pictorial than from the psychological point of view. Pink and pale blue blend subtly in the clothes, making them tremble slightly against the mist-shrouded landscape in the background.

CHAPTER TWELVE

After Saskia's death

Months after Saskia was dead and buried, her image lived on in Rembrandt's mind, and in 1643 she made one last reappearance on canvas. Now that she was no longer there to pose for him, he produced perhaps the most moving portrait of her that he had ever painted. He depicts her with a slight smile, and radiant with an inner life richer than any he had been able to perceive in her face while she lived. Once again he indulged his liking for dressing her up sumptuously and adorning her with pearls and a gold chain, but this no longer appears merely a vain display of precious, futile objects. One is keenly aware that the purpose of the adornment is to show, one last time, how dear she was to him, to bring her back, at least in painting, to that life which she loved when their happiness was in full bloom.

Rembrandt painted himself in the same year, dressed in such a way as to be able to take his place beside Saskia, but the face has the grave look of a man who has recently experienced acute grief. A year or two later he produced a new self-portrait in which his pose recalls that of 1640. The spirit which the painting displays, however, is very different. The costume is less elegant, though by no means shabby, the contour of the beret no longer describes a supple, flexible line, it traces a more tortuous, abrupt and unpredictable course. There is something determined, even rebellious, about it. No longer is Rembrandt concerned to make his face look distinguished: he quite simply presents it as it really is. One can imagine the wrinkles on the brow, which is slightly hidden by the shadow of the beret. The cheeks are no longer firm but puffy. The nose, whose line Rembrandt had fined down in the *Self-Portrait* of 1640, is here shown as it actually was, thick and fleshy. His gaze is penetrating, but one has the impression that, fundamentally, it is not aimed at the spectator. This man is above all communing with himself.

This is not to say that Rembrandt took refuge in sterile solitude. It was during the first half of the 1640s, in fact, that he taught his most gifted pupil, Carel Fabritius. Besides Dutchmen, his students now included four Germans and a Dane (Bernhardt Keil), which confirms that his fame had spread far beyond the borders of his own country. His pupils had their own studio on the top floor of the house, their rooms being subdivided by movable partitions. A drawing which dates from about 1641 shows this *Studio*—a woman can be seen posing for two students, while their master has dropped in for a moment to have a look at their work. It is only natural that Rembrandt's strong personality should have marked those who studied under him, and in fact there are many 17th century Dutch drawings which reveal his influence. There are still others which are variously ascribed to Rembrandt himself or to one of the artists under his guidance.

We have no precise knowledge of how Rembrandt lived in the years immediately following Saskia's death. A reconstruction of his life at this time can only be based on the little information in our possession. Rembrandt was left with Titus who, at the time of his mother's death, was not yet ten months old. Since he could not simultaneously paint, give lessons, and take care of the child, he was forced to call in somebody else to help. The person who was thus introduced into the Rembrandt household was Geertghe Dircx, a trumpeter's widow. She stayed there till 1648, and she was not to leave without a fuss. In the meantime, however, she took care of the child and won Rembrandt's affection and even, so it seems, his love.

69 *Interior of a Studio with a Painter painting the Portrait of a Couple.*
About 1648

There is no clear evidence that she also figured in his art, for it is not possible to identify her with certainty in any of Rembrandt's works.

It is quite possible, however, that the features and gestures of the Virgin in the several versions of *The Holy Family* which Rembrandt painted or drew during this period were Geertghe's own. The choice of this subject is clearly consistent with his own life and the presence of Titus. The drawing which he executed in 1645, showing a melancholy St Joseph sitting behind a table, with the Virgin holding the Child on her lap, must have reproduced attitudes which he had seen and feelings which he had experienced in his own house.

The Holy Family with the Angels, a painting of the same year, is not imbued with such sad thoughts and such a gloomy silence. St Joseph is working, and the Virgin breaks off from reading the Bible

Ill. 70

131

for a moment to turn towards the cradle in which the Child is sleeping. The young woman's facial expression and gesture are full of a most natural tenderness. The whole scene takes place on a strictly human level. Were it not for the descending angels (to whom no one in the picture is paying the least attention) the group would evoke not the Holy Family, but a small craftsman's family obliged by straitened circumstances to live in the very studio where the father works. This is by no means to say that the picture is devoid of religious content, which is to be found in the contemplative fervour with which Rembrandt regards life, rather than in outward signs and accessories. This same quality enabled Rembrandt, in *The Holy Family with the Curtain* in the Gemäldegalerie, Kassel (1646), to leave out the angels and paint what by another artist would merely be a genre scene but which, in this case, is unmistakably a religious picture.

The movement which the angels introduced in the 1645 painting is no longer of the sharp kind that Rembrandt formerly favoured. One no longer has the impression of a spring uncoiling, as in *The Angel leaving Tobit's Family* (1637). These angels descend slowly: they glide through the air, their bodies and wings brushed by a dull light. In addition to curves and diagonals, one is also conscious in this work of stable verticals and horizontals, and the leading angel suggests a straight line which is carried on by the chair and the edge of the cradle. The contrast between verticals and horizontals is even more pronounced in the drawn version of *The Holy Family* which is the very reverse of baroque. Here St Joseph and the Virgin make up two imposing well-balanced pyramids. The kind of cap which the Saint wears and the odd broad flat hat of the Virgin are not merely head-gear. They are the means by which two shapes are contrasted.

Rembrandt also portrayed a small child in certain other paintings of this period—*Joseph's Dream in the Stable at Bethlehem* (1645), *Circumcision*, and two versions of *Adoration of the Shepherds* (1646). These two paintings were produced at the request of the Prince Regent Frederick Henry, who on 29 November 1646 gave orders for 2400 guilders to be paid to Rembrandt for his work. The amount of the payment is interesting, for it indicates that Rembrandt now received twice as much as in 1639. The canvases formed part of the same series and were roughly the same size as the two completed at

70 *The Holy Family with the Angels.* 1645

that date. Unfortunately for Rembrandt the man who was now prepared to pay such generous fees died in 1647 and he was never again called upon to work for the court at the Hague.

Ill. 72   His *Adoration of the Shepherds* is, not unexpectedly, a picture which offers a particularly wide range of possibilities for using chiaroscuro. A dark stable, the small, flickering light of the lanterns, the fact that the artist was free to position them as he pleased—all this combined to make up a subject with which Rembrandt was in his element. Even better for him, he was able to direct this light on to the kind of faces which he loved to paint, faces without conventional prettiness, smooth or bearded, but always homely and expressing simple feelings with sincerity.

The presence of Geertghe Dircx may also have inspired Rembrandt to revert to painting nudes. The model for *Bathsheba at her Toilet*

Ill. 73   (1643), however, is not the same as in *Susannah and the Elders* (1647), about which numerous theories can be advanced but none proved. Whatever the identity of the model, Bathsheba is now more exposed than in the 1632 version, where she modestly displayed only part of her front, and her back. She is also much better proportioned than the nudes of previous years. Susannah, whose third appearance this is in Rembrandt's painting, has a supple, youthful body, and is far and away more attractive than in previous versions. As far as the elders are concerned, the one who is trying to uncover the frightened Susannah completely—he is not in fact particularly old—can be traced back to a vigorous drawing of some ten years before, while the other

Ill. 71   recalls *The Oriental* whom Rembrandt portrayed in 1635. He owed the framework of his composition, the garden on the right and the building in the background, to Lastman, who had painted the same subject. Rembrandt's painting, however, is more concentrated than his former teacher's, and also less anecdotal and less theatrical. The semi-darkness of the landscape shows up Susannah's light body, emphasizing the chilliness of her naked form and the qualities which make it so disturbing for the two men.

Bathsheba and *Susannah and the Elders* are not the only themes of which Rembrandt produced two or three versions. In 1645 he reverted to the story of Tobit, which had already inspired previous works in 1626, 1636 and 1637. In actual fact, Rembrandt did not always

Ill. 10   represent the same episode. While the first painting showed Tobit's

71 *Oriental.* 1632–36

wife bringing a goat which the blind man believes to be stolen, the next dealt with *Tobias healing his Father* and the third and last with *The Angel leaving Tobit's family.* It was to the first of these scenes that Rembrandt now returned, but the new work had nothing in common with the old. There is now no trace of exaggeration, and both gestures and expressions are simple. The light is no longer harsh, it is shaded off subtly in a room spacious enough to contain its languorous progress. The bodies have lost their previous clumsiness; they are less sharply drawn and have more spiritual life.

The new version of *Christ at Emmaus* which Rembrandt executed in 1648 provides an even better yardstick by which to measure his progress since his early years. This time Christ is facing towards the front of the picture, as in Leonardo's *Last Supper.* The way in which he breaks the bread is as unspectacular as possible. The gestures of the disciples are also very restrained, and their astonishment by no means

73 *Susannah and the Elders.* 1647

betokens fright. The composition is almost symmetrical, but the characters are placed at a table and in front of a recess, neither of which
occupies a central position. Although the picture recalls Italian art,
Rembrandt avoids the rigourously symmetrical order which Leonardo
and Raphael are so fond of using. The work bears traces of classical
influence, but Rembrandt once again demonstrates a desire to interpret his models in his own personal way. This is also apparent in the
architecture. The pilasters which frame the recess and the arch which
marks its upper limit serve only to make the characters look bigger,
and they enclose a huge area of shadow in front of which shines the
brilliant figure of Christ. By contrast to the works of Leonardo and

137

◁ 72 *Adoration of the Shepherds.* 1646

Raphael, then, the architecture here has no independent value. It is not arresting in the harmony of its proportions or its majesty, instead it is completely filled with spiritual significance. The same is true of the light. It is most brilliant on the table-cloth, thus providing Christ with a kind of pedestal of light which immediately draws attention to him. Two-thirds of the picture is 'empty', a painted surface animated only by gradations of ochre and brown.

The Good Samaritan which hangs in the Louvre is no longer attributed to Rembrandt, but to one of his pupils, since cleaning revealed that the signature on the picture was forged. The fact remains that this is a fine painting, and that Rembrandt illustrated the same parable in drawings. Among them is a wash-drawing in the British Museum, which portrays the arrival at the inn in the evening. This drawing has an especially exciting richness about it. The light is bright enough to make the Samaritan and the characters carrying in the wounded man stand out in the darkness, but also sufficiently soft to preserve the velvety mystery of the night.

As far as portraiture was concerned, Rembrandt produced in 1642—1643 what appears to be a series of studies of old men's heads drawn with the brush. The size of these works is generally small, and they were executed at speed. In actual fact, these works are more reminiscent of his Leyden period than his early years in Amsterdam, since the search for expression takes precedence over all other considerations.

Other portraits of the period, which were clearly commissioned, are in the same line of descent as the preceding works. Some of them, for instance, *A Falconer* and its companion picture, *Portrait of a Lady with a Fan*, can be more especially linked to his *Self-Portrait* of 1640. They are distinguished by an unostentatious elegance. In addition, the reproduction of the fabrics is plainly more important to Rembrandt than the rendering of his sitters' personalities—the faces are flat and without much individual character.

In other portraits, the face is the arresting feature. The portrait thought to be of the theologian Jan C. Sylvius, the husband of one of Saskia's cousins, may not really depict this character at all, for he died in 1638, and the picture was not executed until 1644 or 1645 (although the possibility that this was a posthumous portrait cannot be ruled out, especially as Sylvius appeared in an etching of 1646). At any rate, this is a man whose face and gaze reveal a mind which categorically rejects anything that might distract it from its austere, speculative thought. Though Rembrandt does not stress the characterization, his sitter has more personality than the preacher Johannes Uytenbogaert in a portrait painted ten years previously and far more carefully executed.

Rembrandt also continued to portray Jewish models with much feeling. Sometimes these portraits are merely half-length and he concentrates on the face, on other occasions he also shows their long, slender hands. While he uses rich clothing to stress the dignity which they possess or which he wishes to give them, Rembrandt is now less concerned than in previous works with the picturesque and the exotic. He makes their expressions more reserved but simultaneously gives them a more profound inner life.

Although Rembrandt always preferred to paint the wrinkled faces of old people, there were other occasions on which he portrayed the head of a child or of a girl. Rarely, however, do these characters look really young; one constantly has the feeling that the seriousness and sternness which they display are on the point of turning into surliness. In 1645, however, he portrayed a *Young Girl leaning on a Window-Sill*, whose round face has a touching freshness. Her gaze may be *Ill. 74* serious and distant, but the expression is charming, more so than that of Saskia portrayed in a similar pose. Rembrandt now showed himself also capable of perceiving a moving life in faces not yet marked with age. It would probably be more correct to say that he was able to endow them with this life, that his own personality had reached a stage of development which enabled him to bestow its riches on everything to which he turned his attention.

·74 *Young Girl leaning on a Window-Sill.* 1645

CHAPTER THIRTEEN

Essential reality

In the year following Saskia's death, Rembrandt etched one of his finest landscapes, *The Three Trees*. It has greater pathos than previous landscape prints, which comes as no surprise when one considers a slightly older drawing, in pen-and-ink touched up with wash, which portrays *Cottages under a stormy Sky*. Already, in this work, there are clouds rising in the sky, threatening to cover it completely, while the uneasy light on the thatched roofs, the ground, and the foliage of the trees is locked in by dense shadows. In *The Three Trees*, the contrast between light and dark is even more intense, complex and subtle. The effect which Rembrandt had sought to achieve in his paintings, which he had thought he could only reach by composing imaginary, more or less fantastic landscapes, he captured here by portraying one of the most common types of Dutch countryside—a plain intersected by canals, people working in the fields, cows grazing in the meadows, a town in the distance, water, and on a hill more to the foreground,

Ill. 75

Ill. 77

75 *The Three Trees.* 1643

three oak-trees without the heroic look which he generally gave trees in his paintings. The very ordinariness of the scene makes the work more moving, as it illustrates Rembrandt's power to transform his subjects.

The alternation of zones of light and darkness to the left suggests an area of vast proportions. The eye has the impression of traversing an immense space before finally arriving at the thin, luminous strip of water wedged between earth and sky. This very high sky is animated by a whole range of lines, from dots and light, thin strokes to whirling curves and oblique lines firmly drawn in with a ruler. The impending triumph of darkness and distress makes the light even

76 *Six's Bridge.* 1645

77 *Cottages under a stormy Sky.* 1640–43

more brilliant. The shadows are deep and wide on the earth, and have already enveloped the trees, except for a few condemned gleams of light which flicker in the wind. Rarely in the history of art has a landscape combined observation of the outside world and expression of human sensibilities so well, without losing its realism and becoming completely transformed by the artist's vision.

Rembrandt was no more a man of one style and one state of mind at this stage of his life than he ever had been. He experienced sadness and mental anguish, but there were also hours, and no doubt days, when he knew peace of mind, and different subjects came equally naturally to him. Thus not all his etched landscapes have the pathos of *The Three Trees* nor are all so pervaded and transfigured by his feelings. *Six's Bridge,* for example, is merely a brisk, concise nota-tion of a scene, a peaceful world bathed by an even light, unfolding under a cloudless sky.

Ill. 76

While some of Rembrandt's drawings bear a relation to this etch-ing, others echo the dramatic atmosphere of *Cottages under a stormy Sky.* At this stage of his career he seems to have been frequently attracted by the countryside. A farm on the edge of a forest flooded by sunlight, sand-hills with scanty vegetation, a village covered in snow, a canal with dwellings huddled among the trees behind it— Rembrandt set all these scenes down on paper, sometimes adding thick patches of wash to the impetuously scribbled lines.

Geographer seated at a Writing-Table (1645) is similar in style to *Cottages under a stormy Sky* but here the contrast between light and dark is more pronounced, the lines have more fluidity and the medium tones are perhaps softer. *Geographer seated at a Writing-Table* pre-sents the theme of a character in a room, which rarely appears in Rembrandt's paintings, except when he depicts a biblical figure— Tobit, an Apostle, the Holy Family or an imaginary theologian or philosopher. In any case, Rembrandt never showed any inclination to paint interiors along the lines of Vermeer or Terborch, Pieter de Hooch or Jan Steen, showing people of the 17th century in their natural surroundings with the costumes and pursuits of their time. He did not even do so at the very start of his career in Leyden, for both *The Musicians* and *The Money-Changer* lack the realism (some-times pervaded by a poetic atmosphere) which characterized the art of those painters. Nevertheless several of the drawings which he

144

78 *Landscape with a Road between the Trees.* 1652–55

79 *Landscape with Trees.* 1650–55

executed during the 1630s made use of this theme and his portraits of Saskia in bed did, after all, depict the interior in a fairly objective spirit.

In *Geographer seated at a Writing-Table*, however, the description of the room is only summary, and the geographer seems rather to be one of Rembrandt's imaginary scholars than someone he had actually seen. This man looks like an old, bearded patriarch. He is neither examining a map nor looking at the globe which stands before him on the table, but contemplating the light coming in through the window. In other words he is concentrating on the intangible, the immeasurable, and this is clearly for him the essential reality. The globe, the books, objects in general, have little more than a phantom existence. This geographer is obsessed by something other than the immediate instruments of his work. He appears to be meditating more on the mysteries of creation than on the world's external appearance. The most vividly lit part of the picture is his clothing, not his face.

Interiors appear not only in Rembrandt's drawings but also in his etchings. His print of *The Gold-Weigher* (1639) had already featured an interior, although it is true that greater emphasis was laid on the anecdotal aspect of the scene than on the atmosphere in the room. He depicts the weighing operation, showing the weigher's assistants, the small sacks which one guesses are full of gold, the scales leaning under the weight of a sack, the register in which the weight is to be recorded, some small casks and a chest. Rembrandt strives to make his description plausible, and does his best to reproduce the substance of each object.

Ill. 80   This last concern is not totally lacking in *Jan Six reading*, an etching of 1647, but here other considerations are more important. Jan Six belonged to a rich family of Amsterdam merchants. At the time of this etching he was 29 years old; later on, at the age of 73, he was to become burgomaster of the city. In the meantime he wrote poetry and cultivated his mind. Rembrandt, who was a friend of Six's, took great care over the image which he presented of him. Six is portrayed looking down at a book, his left arm leaning on the window; the curtains have been drawn back, so that a vibrant back-lighting shines out behind him. His hair is so drenched with light that it looks like a whitish foam. The face and the left hand are also very bright, while occasional softer patches of light also appear in the room, which

146

otherwise is dominated by dark grey and black. Certain objects can still be made out, but they are unobtrusive; the eye is drawn to the character, who is not to be distracted from his book by all the brightness of the outside world.

Reading was one of the themes which Dutch painters of the 17th century interpreted on various different occasions. It inspired Terborch and Vermeer to produce some notable works of quiet, delicate poetry. Yet in the case of these artists, the reading matter is normally letters, and the letter always evokes the person who has written it as well as the relationship between the writer and the reader, who is generally a woman. Hence there is the intrusion, however subtle, of anecdote. Jan Six, however, is reading a book. The relationship in the picture is entirely between the text and his mind. We do not ask ourselves what the text is about or who it is written by; we see only the reality of the reading which concentrates, illuminates, and enraptures Six's mind.

About 1648, Rembrandt began to etch another interior, this time an artist's studio, in which he intended to portray *The Sketcher and his Model*. The work was never to be completed. Only a few lines allow the sketcher, who is sitting facing almost full-on, the naked woman, who is standing with her back towards us, and the various objects which are placed in the foreground, to stand out quietly from the white paper. In the upper part of the etching, on the other hand, the draughtsmanship is more elaborate: here everything is represented in depth, and the substance of each object is made apparent, together with the silent life it leads in the semi-darkness. A preparatory drawing in the British Museum reveals what the definitive arrangement of whites, blacks and greys was to have been. Here the nude is bathed in light, and stands out distinctly against the background, while the easel, which becomes so dazzlingly white in the print, is darker in the drawing. The sketcher is a dark mass flecked with gleams of light and streaked with vigorously drawn lines. He looks like a hunter on the prowl ducking in order to make certain that his prey will not escape. The etching does not show the same tension in the relationship between the artist and his model, but it is not without eloquence. The strokes which appear to be roaming around to no purpose are still forceful; however casual they may sometimes look, they suggest objects by marking as many features

80 *Jan Six reading.* 1647

as are necessary to give them an individual appearance. There is nothing schematic about the way in which the nude is drawn. Rembrandt conjures up the woman's body with extremely light, sensitive draughtsmanship. Even the whiteness of the skin, which is so unused

148

81 *Self-portrait (Rembrandt drawing). 1648*

to being exposed to the light, stands out well, despite the scarcity of contrasts.

Whereas in this print the sketcher remains anonymous (although his attitude and his burning eyes are most expressive), in another

Ill. 81

etching of 1648 the artist can be identified explicitly as Rembrandt himself. In this new *Self-Portrait,* Rembrandt is positioned behind a table by a window, lit by bright daylight. The light which reaches the face, however, is quite gentle. It moulds the features firmly but not sharply. Rembrandt no longer wishes to evoke a reader whose mind is elsewhere, as in *Jan Six,* but to show a creator at work, and, since he wants to make his presence strongly felt, he dispenses with everything which might divert attention from him. There are no curtains on the windows, no object in the room on which the light might play. There is hardly any feeling about the room or the material of the cloth covering the table which, in other etchings, is reconstituted with great thoroughness. Nor is the clothing of a kind to attract attention by its elegance. In fact, there is nothing distracting in the entire work. The bust of Rembrandt resembles a squat pyramid. His face is bloated, his expression not very friendly, his gaze intent and solemn. The determination, intractability and stubbornness of the face are accentuated by the hat. One must remember that this is the portrait of a man of 42, for he looks easily another ten years older.

Ill. 82

Two etchings in which Rembrandt showed particular interest in the spatial construction of an interior also date from 1648. One of them is entitled *Medea, or the Marriage of Jason and Creusa.* This particular episode in Greek mythology has inspired few artists and Rembrandt himself would certainly never have had the idea of handling the theme had Jan Six not written, and wished to publish, a tragedy entitled *Medea* for which this etching was to serve as a frontispiece. Moreover, he made no effort to give either his heroes or the architecture a specifically Greek appearance. The characters are crowded together in a kind of temple whose roof is supported by high columns and whose various parts are lit in different ways. The variety of levels adds to the complexity of the geometrical elements which give the composition its forceful arrangement.

Ill. 83

The second of these prints portrays *Jews in the Synagogue* and here space is ordered much more simply, strictly according to the rules of Italian perspective. Thus he entirely omits the ceiling, no doubt so that the vanishing-lines which run towards the bottom of the print can be clearly seen. The progressive reduction in size of the characters also helps to create the illusion of perceptible depth. The systematic nature of the composition would be blatantly obvious but for the

82 *Medea, or the Marriage of Jason and Creusa.* 1648

83 *Jews in the Synagogue.* 1648

play of light and shade which serves to disguise it. The human interest which attaches to the old men is another aid to concealment. For these majestic frail beings with their rather fantastic dress are not 17th century figures. They immediately catch our imagination and almost prevent us from noticing that Rembrandt is concerned with more than simply rendering attitudes and facial expressions.

CHAPTER FOURTEEN

Hendrickje

In 1648 the treaty of Münster put an end to the Thirty Years War. It also confirmed Dutch independence. The King of Spain was obliged to recognize formally that the Netherlands were henceforth free and sovereign. Although this event was of considerable importance in the political and economic spheres, its repercussions in the art world were extremely limited. This is neither surprising nor regrettable when one considers *The Banquet offered to the Civic Guard on the Occasion of the Peace of Münster* by Bartholomeus van der Helst and *The Oath of Peace at Münster* by Gerard Terborch. Van der Helst remained true to himself, that is to say skilful but tedious, and Terborch has fortunately left us with works which are less stilted and more poetic than this historical painting.

There is no reason why Rembrandt should have commemorated this event. Nobody now wanted to commission him for a *Banquet* or a second *Night Watch*. When, shortly before Münster, Princess Amalia de Solms, widow of the Prince Regent Frederick Henry, selected half-a-dozen painters to execute works intended to glorify her husband, not even Constantijn Huygens seems to have made

84 *Portrait of Hendrickje Stoffels.* 1652

85 *Portrait of Hendrickje Stoffels.* 1658–59

representations on his behalf. It was now universally understood that Rembrandt could be relied upon for an individual portrait or a religious composition but that it was best not to come to him for a historical painting or an allegory. Besides, it is reasonable to believe that Rembrandt himself shared this opinion and was happy to be forgotten when work of this kind was being distributed. *The Concord of the State* had not been an encouraging attempt. He unfailingly preferred subjects dictated to him by his own inspiration only.

Ill. 81   We have already seen that, in the etched *Self-Portrait* of 1648, Rembrandt looks older than he actually was. This premature ageing may have been the result of hard work, but the more likely cause is the difficulties of his private life. Documents of 1649 reveal that he was confronted with new worries in that year, but it may safely be assumed that he had already had troubles for some time. The frequency with which these worries occurred was sufficient to undermine the stoutest of constitutions; they beset him in his own house, in his own family circle.

The cause of all these troubles was Geertghe Dircx, the woman he had taken into his service after Saskia's death. In the early stages she seems to have discharged her duties well. She must even have had a considerable affection for Titus, since on 25 January 1648 she made him her residuary legatee. Later on the situation deteriorated, and it was decided that she should leave the house. Rembrandt promised to pay her 150 guilders a year, on condition that she in no way alter the provisions of her will in Titus' favour. The artist had given her presents, and in particular a diamond ring which had probably belonged to Saskia and which he no doubt wished to be returned to his son one day. For this reason he promised, on learning that Geertghe had pawned some of these presents, to give her sufficient money for them to be redeemed, even raising his original offer of 150 guilders to 200. The housekeeper did not agree to these proposed arrangements and took Rembrandt to court over it. She declared that Rembrandt had been her lover and that he had promised to marry her. The artist did not answer the first two summonses, as he still hoped to reach a direct agreement with her. In the end he appeared in court, and on 23 October 1649 he was ordered to pay her the sum of 200 guilders a year. This was not the last chapter in this sorry episode. Having lost control of her nerves, Geertghe was later to lose control of her reason too. She then had to be confined to a mental hospital and Rembrandt had to advance money to meet the cost of her upkeep.

All these details are known to us through documents which have been preserved. Rembrandt's biographers have felt bound to take these into consideration, particularly as the documentary material relating to his private life is so sparse. For instance, there is no document of this period which reveals the place that another woman had taken in his home and his affection. Yet this woman, Hendrickje Stoffels, meant more to him in every way than Geertghe Dircx.

Houbraken, the author of a work on Dutch painters which appeared early in the 18th century, described her as 'a peasant woman from Ransdorp'. It is impossible to establish with any accuracy her age at the time she first entered Rembrandt's service. She is believed to have been born somewhere between 1623 and 1626 and to have been already installed in Rembrandt's house before Geertghe's departure. It may indeed have been her presence which explained this departure, provoking jealous scenes leading to the final rupture. For Hendrickje seems to have won her master's affection quickly, and it was to be a deep affection which she would never lose.

The fact that Rembrandt, after marrying an aristocrat, should fall in love with a humble servant girl, and avow this love, is one more proof of how little importance he now attached to his fellow-citizens' regard. Quite clearly, there was no longer any point of contact between the rules by which they lived and his own, between their concern for respectability and his need for sincerity and truth. He had loved the woman in Saskia but had perhaps also appreciated her social position and her fortune. With Hendrickje, he loved only the human qualities—her physical but above all else 'her personal attributes. The portraits of Hendrickje are consequently different from those of Saskia. Hendrickje is dressed more plainly, although she is sometimes to be seen wearing jewels. Rembrandt was not concerned with outward display. He wished instead to show the goodness of the woman, her unselfishness and the affection which she brought to him.

In the oldest of these portraits, which hangs in the Louvre *Ill. 84* (c. 1652), he emphasizes the oval shape of the face and moulds it with great delicacy. In the portrait in the Alte Pinakothek, Munich (c. 1655), the outline of the head is more wavy, and the

86 *Hendrickje Stoffels in Bed.* 1657

87 *Bathsheba at her Toilet.* 1654

features are given a slightly blurred appearance by the alternation of light and shade on the face. Hendrickje is thus fairly unobtrusive, as she must have been in everyday life, but her human qualities are obvious. The painting in the Staatliche Museen, Berlin-Dahlem *Ill. 85*

c. 1658/59), by contrast, is lit in such a way that sharp relief is combined with strongly marked features. Hendrickje appears at the recess of a window, the very picture of devotion. Although she wears ear-rings and a pearl bracelet, her necklace and her dress are plain. But the painting immensely ennobles and enriches this dress. Its ordinariness is barely noticeable, so attractive is the grave sonority of reds and browns, the richness of the material, the breadth and vigour of the draughtsmanship.

Rembrandt not only portrayed Hendrickje's face, but also, on two separate occasions in 1654, her body. In *A Woman bathing* it can be seen only in part and in a pose which could hardly be less elegant. She is wading cautiously into the water, clad only in a long shift which she holds up in such a position that the lower part of her abdomen is just concealed. There is an oddly rich look about the red and gold dress which she has just taken off, but the shift seems to be cut in a coarse, stiff cloth. Neither its material nor its shape, made even more ugly by the very low neckline, helps to give this body the least attraction. Yet *A Woman bathing* is one of those works which are not forgotten. What in another painter's version might have been a spectacle for voyeurs, or at the very least have bordered on the licentious, does not here convey a suspicion of eroticism or indecency. This is another example of Rembrandt's straightforward observation of real life. His handling of the subject is so earnest that vulgarity and impropriety are avoided. Once again the treatment is lively and accurate. Broad brush-strokes enliven the whites and greys of the shift, and contrasting with this are the mat tints of the face and the upper body, the ashy pinks of the legs, the browns of the background, and finally the red and gold of the dress, which are also reflected in the water.

Ill. 87   The second of these pictures *Bathsheba at her Toilet,* displays a similar colouring and approach. Here the body is completely naked, a young, quite firm, not particularly graceful, but also not unattractive body. As in the previous painting, the model is not concerned for her body to be shown to advantage. We surprise her in an intimate moment when she does not feel exposed to the gaze of an onlooker. A maidservant is bent over one of her feet wiping the toes, and she carries out this humble task with a seriousness normally reserved for religious ceremonies.

Rubens also produced a version of this subject. In his case, not unexpectedly, the servant has a more noble occupation than the foot-cleaning operation in Rembrandt's picture (she is combing Bathsheba's silky hair) while Bathsheba herself seems very conscious of the effect her charms can produce. She looks at the little black boy who brings her David's message not with surprise but with the expression of one who sees a secret wish coming true. Rembrandt's Bathsheba has a sad, suffering look. The letter which she holds in her hand could equally well be the one which informs her of her husband's death as the one asking her to go to David. He clearly was anxious, however, to convey the impression of a woman involved in a drama. Her troubled feelings as she contemplates her fate are quite as easily discernible as her naked body.

In the very year when Hendrickje posed for this picture, her own fate was occupying the thoughts of certain people in Amsterdam. That she should be living with a man who was not her lawful husband obviously did not meet with general approval, particularly as his critics suspected that the reason behind Rembrandt's refusal to regularize his position was financial—he was to hold Saskia's inheritance in usufruct only so long as he did not remarry. In 1654 the two sinners were consequently summoned to appear before the consistory of the Calvinist Church of Amsterdam to give an explanation for their union, which irritated their decent neighbours. As they failed to answer this summons, the consistory repeated the charge at the beginning of July, this time citing only Hendrickje. Biographers of Rembrandt have deduced from this that the court had discovered in the meantime that he was not a member of the national church. Baldinucci even relates that the artist had joined the Mennonite sect, which is possible but not proven. Hendrickje was to receive a third summons and the local friars even had to come to her house to remonstrate with her before she finally agreed, at the end of July, to appear before the ecclesiastical judges. When she made no attempt to deny her liaison with Rembrandt, she was admonished, called upon to repent, and debarred from receiving Holy Communion. Despite the censures she received and the penalties inflicted upon her, however, she remained faithful to her love. Moreover, three months later she gave birth to a girl, who was given the name Cornelia, a name which two other daughters of Rembrandt had already borne, but for

88 *Self-portrait.* 1652

89 *Portrait of Titus at the Writing Desk.* 1655

a few weeks only. The third Cornelia was sturdier than Saskia's children. She grew up along with Titus, and Hendrickje was as much of a mother for him as for her daughter.

It was at about this time that Titus began to be portrayed by his father. Prior to that he had appeared only among other characters and with features which were not strongly marked—in a *Holy Family*, for instance. But now that he was thirteen or fourteen his face was sufficiently interesting for Rembrandt to make him the sole subject of a series of pictures. In one portrait, Titus is seen with his brightly-lit face framed by light, silky hair, his angelic charm

Ill. 89   increased by his fragility. In another he is shown in serious thought, holding a pen over a few sheets of paper: his features, from the semi-darkness, giving the impression not of a face of flesh and blood, but of something between tangible physical reality and the evanescence of a spirit. The head stands out against the background like a star in the night. It is supremely gentle, yet disturbing: one is very conscious of the threat which hangs over childhood, the vulnerability of a young life, the anxiety which the precariousness of the human condition arouses in Rembrandt. In another portrait, Titus' features are less insecure. The emphasis is placed on the comforting beauty of a delicate, sensitive, well-proportioned face, where the gaze has a frankness which even the shadow cannot perturb.

How did the author of these works see himself at this time? The

Ill. 88   man in the *Self-Portrait* of 1652 is obviously as sturdy as an oak, whose strength is needed to brave the storms. He no longer wears his beret at the rather cheeky angle of the 1645 *Self-Portrait*. Now the only purpose of the beret is to shelter the eyes from the light and, symbolically, to protect the head from the blows which he knows will not be spared him. There is nothing assertive about this figure. He is a man on the defensive, and he is strengthened in this by a belief that certain calamities are inevitable, certain misfortunes are part and parcel of human life, especially the life of an artist whose philosophy is not shared by all his fellows.

164

CHAPTER FIFTEEN

Intimations of mortality

During this period Rembrandt did not only paint himself and those of his family circle. In 1651, for instance, he produced a new version of *Young Girl at a Window*. Her round face and inquisitive look do not have the uneasy, disturbing qualities of *Portrait of Titus at the Writing-Desk*. The flesh is not so eaten away that it seems to have changed in substance. Yet behind this chubby face one detects the first signs of an uneasiness which age will only accentuate. For Rembrandt, indeed, this is the lot of all men, the most obvious acquisition of those who have known the passage of time. In his so-called *Portrait of Adriaen van Rijn* (1650), his *Portrait of an old Jew* (1651) or his *Jacob seated* and *Man with a golden Helmet*, both of which date from around 1652, one may find tenacity, resignation, or a slight bitterness, but uneasiness too is an ever-present factor.

Ill. 90

Yet however arresting the psychological aspect of, for example, *Man in a golden Helmet* may be, the attention which Rembrandt lavished on the helmet must also be taken into account if the artist is to be properly understood. The tints of the gold, the play of the light on the reliefs and in the hollows of the ornamental design, the sharply defined light patches and the deep shadows, all these things

90 *Portrait of Adriaen van Rijn.* 1650

91 *Tobit and his Wife spinning at her Wheel.* 1650

were clearly as important for Rembrandt as the face, to which the half-light gives an even more mysterious appearance.

Again, in his *Portrait of Jan Six* (1654), it is the face which commands instant attention, for the expression, seemingly that of a man of 50, although in fact the model was only 36, is immediately arresting. The uneasy light which Rembrandt now cast on almost all faces reveals disillusionment and weariness. But the face makes up only one part of this work which, as well as being a magnificent portrait, is also a pictorial creation of splendid maturity. Quite clearly, Rembrandt executed this picture with as much freedom as a self-portrait. He even gave the colouring a sonority which he no longer sought in his own portraits. The grey jacket, which is set off by yellow buttons and white collar and sleeves, contrasts with a coat whose red is enhanced by ochre lapels. In addition, a jet-black hat contrasts with the face and the light brown hair. As in the finest works of the time, the style is sweeping. The gloves are treated in the broad but powerfully evocative manner typical of Frans Hals towards the end of his life. There are some very bold touches which, seen from close up, look almost unrelated to the rest, but when viewed from a distance, the image of the gloves adds to the magic of the painting as a whole.

We have already seen that Rembrandt, when not producing portraits, usually returned to biblical subjects. Thus, in 1650, he took up the story of Tobit for the fifth time. It will be recalled that in the four previous paintings he had always portrayed an activity, although the episode had not always been the same—Anna bringing the goat, the son healing his father, the angel suddenly flying away. *Ill. 91* Now Rembrandt merely depicted two silent people in their room. Tobit's wife is seated by the window, busy with her spinning, while he is sitting in an armchair, his back turned to the daylight which his blindness in any case would prevent him from seeing. In front of his face is darkness, at his feet a fire which he can only feel. A soft light bathes his head. Although the brilliant rays of light from the world outside are no longer perceptible to his eye, his inner world is not in darkness. His thoughts range all the more freely now that there is nothing to distract them. Physical infirmity has led to spiritual strength.

Two other canvases of the 1650s featured blind characters—*Aristotle contemplating the Bust of Homer* (1653) and *Jacob blessing his* *Ill. 92* *Grandchildren* (1656). The first of these subjects is an unexpected one for Rembrandt who, if he possessed busts of Homer and Aristotle, never seems to have set great store by Greek philosophy, or any other sort, for that matter. In any case, with his broad cap, his velvet tunic and a kind of surplice covering his shoulders and his arms, Rembrandt's Aristotle looks more like a rabbi or a Father of the Church than an ancient Greek philosopher. But such considerations are quibbles: this is a character who is meditating about man and about life, which for Rembrandt was the important thing.

What answers does Aristotle hope to find in the idealized portrait of the blind poet? Not content with giving him a searching look, he places his hand on the head as though touching might bring him the realization of a truth which eludes the sight. The scene is both sad and solemn. It reproduces a disappointing monologue, but it also shows all the nobility which meditative thought can confer on a human being. This nobility is emphasized by the colouring which, with its dark blacks, its yellowish light patches and its sparkling golds, is both sumptuous and austere.

This work was commissioned from Rembrandt by a Sicilian art-collector, Antonio Ruffo da Messina. Two more commissions followed from the same source—*Alexander the Great* and *Homer*. The second of these is still in existence (see below), but *Alexander the Great*, unless destroyed, has yet to be found. It has been suggested that this work should be identified with a picture in the Art Gallery, Glasgow, in which a character in armour can be seen wearing a helmet adorned by an owl. The theory has not been proved, however, and the character in question has been diversely interpreted as being, among others, Athena, St Michael, Mars, Bellona and Apollo.

Shortly after painting *Aristotle*, Rembrandt had a disagreement with a Portuguese merchant by the name of Diego Andrada, who engaged him to paint the portrait of a girl. Andrada put down 75 guilders in advance and pledged himself to pay the rest when the picture was completed. When he saw it, however, he found it bore no resemblance whatever to the model and demanded that Rembrandt should make certain modifications. To this the artist replied that he had no intention of altering it until he received the balance of the money or a security. When that had been done, he would take the canvas along to the Guild of St Luke and would only be prepared to change it if, in the Guild's opinion, it was not a true likeness. He added that, in the event that Andrada did not accept this proposal, he would keep the picture, finish it when the opportunity offered and sell it when he decided to organize a public auction of his works. The document which records this quarrel does not reveal the reaction of the Portuguese merchant. In all probability Rembrandt persisted with his uncompromising attitude, for he could not abide clients trying to impose their demands on him.

The blind character in *Jacob blessing his Grandchildren* is neither *Ill. 92* as impassive as the bust of Homer, nor as passive as Tobit—he takes decisive action. Jacob should normally have placed his right hand on the head of the elder boy, Manasseh, and not, as he did, on the head

92 Jacob blessing his Grandchildren. 1656

of Ephraim. According to the Bible, Joseph was displeased by this gesture, and attempted to rectify it by explaining to Jacob that he had made a mistake. In Rembrandt's picture Joseph plays only a minor part in the proceedings. Far from revealing displeasure, his expression is respectful and peaceful, as also is his wife's and Ephraim's. On this point, then, Rembrandt's account of the scene diverges from the Scriptures in order to make it immediately clear that Jacob is directed by a superior force, which it is useless to try and resist.

The harmony which exists between the characters is repeated in the colours and shapes. Jacob, Joseph and the two children form what is

93 *Christ and the Woman of Samaria.* 1655

almost an equilateral triangle, and inside this triangle the colouring is delicate and light. At different points it is warmer, or colder and duller, but all the shades blend in with each other. The same combination of tints appears in the face of the woman in the brown dress who stands a little to one side, her body describing the shape of an isosceles triangle. The blanket on the bed introduces a broad band of red, but there is nothing garish about it, and it harmonizes well with the deep browns and the delicate radiance of the light tints.

Ill. 93 Whereas the composition of this picture is based on the interplay of triangles, in *Christ and the Woman of Samaria* (1655), in the Staatliche Museen, Berlin-Dahlem, it rests on the contrast between verticals and horizontals. Here, indeed, the geometrical structure has an obviousness seldom to be found in Rembrandt's work, especially in his paintings. Yet it is not the only factor to give order to the picture. Chiaroscuro also has an important part, now showing up the bone-structure and now playing it down, so that it is really the most expressive element in the painting.

The light shimmers in the sky, on the landscape, and behind Jacob's well, which is nothing more than a dark mass. Above the well, in the centre of the canvas and against the light, can be seen the upper half of the Samaritan woman's body, while Christ is positioned near the edge of the picture, in the shadow. The light between the two characters seems to be getting brighter and spreading wider, but the woman is not aware of it, she heeds only the words which are addressed to her from the shadow and which are so shrouded in darkness that her mind can only gradually comprehend their full meaning. The attitudes are extremely simple, yet it is immediately evident that there is nothing commonplace about this meeting; this whispered dialogue in the silence of the late evening is no empty exchange of words.

But what are we supposed to make of that strange work known as *The Polish Rider*, which Rembrandt executed around 1655? The horse in this work is different from any other to be found in his compositions, including the one in his *Equestrian Portrait of Frederick Rihel* (c. 1649), where Rembrandt, adhering to the usual formula of baroque painting for this kind of subject, portrayed the rider with an expression of proud, complacent assurance, his mount rearing beneath him. In complete contrast, the horse of *The Polish Rider* has an uncommonly emaciated appearance, as though it has had to make a gruelling journey through vast barren deserts—what is more, it looks condemned to continue its travels until it finally collapses exhausted to the ground. Where has the horse come from and where is it going to in this darkening landscape? What is the significance of this unknown horseman, and what fate awaits him? What is the scene which the young man leaves behind him, from which he cannot even avert his eyes?

This painting has been compared with a drawing by Rembrandt, showing the skeletons of a knight and a horse, which he may have seen in a *theatrum anatomicum* in Leyden or Amsterdam. Yet this drawing does not explain the picture, which ultimately must remain enigmatic. Indeed, enigma seems to be one of its essential components. It places the two figures in the realm of fable, to which Rembrandt always inclined, not because he wished to flee reality, but because he sought to make it more intense than in the world of ordinary life.

The idea of death inherent in this skeleton of a horse became a reality in another work of the same period, *The slaughtered Ox*. *Ill. 94* Rembrandt was not the first to paint a butchered carcass. Almost a century before, the Flemish artist Joachim Beuckelaer had portrayed a pig in a similar state to this ox, while before that Beuckelaer's master, Pieter Aertsen, had painted a butcher's stall and its contents in considerable detail. Rembrandt himself was no newcomer to the theme of the recently slaughtered animal. Around 1638 he had painted a series of dead birds, in 1643 he had produced an etching of a slaughtered hog, while a first version of *The slaughtered Ox* (Art Gallery, Glasgow) had been in existence since the late 1640s. However, the 1655 picture, which hangs in the Louvre, is the finer version of this subject.

Rembrandt makes us intensely aware of the poignant qualities of the beast's eviscerated carcass and the bare flesh given up to the butcher's axe. But the painting transforms this painful reality into a work of art. This transformation is so obvious that in the last resort it dominates all else. It is difficult to think of death when confronted by those rich whitish yellows, pinks, and reds which reveal the flavour of Rembrandt's palette. Rembrandt's ability to transform his subjects completely has already been remarked upon, but perhaps nowhere is it better displayed than in this picture. He takes this stiff,

94 *The slaughtered Ox.* 1655

pallid, blood-stained carcass and gives it a magnificent pictorial impact.

Death also occupies a central position in *The Anatomy Lesson of Dr. Deyman* (1656). Only a fragment of this work remains, as it was partially destroyed in a fire. However a preparatory drawing reveals the original composition—fairly symmetrical, and more clearly arranged than *The Anatomy Lesson of Dr. Tulp*. Whether it was also more moving is difficult to judge, but certainly the fragment which has been preserved is rather cold. The corpse slicing through space at a perpendicular angle is too reminiscent of Mantegna's *Dead Christ*; it looks too much like an exercise in style; the large feet which loom up in the foreground seem a little too grotesque to be really moving. It would be tempting to conclude that Rembrandt is more moving when he paints the carcass of an animal than when he portrays the corpse of a man. Yet it must not be forgotten that he executed the first canvas on his own account, while the second was commissioned by a client. Rembrandt may have accepted a commission of this kind for reasons of prestige or for reasons of a financial order, or possibly a combination of the two—in 1656, as we shall see, it would have been quite natural for Rembrandt to feel the need for both money and prestige.

95 The Hundred-Guilder Print. 1649

CHAPTER SIXTEEN

The master-etcher

During the period in which he executed the paintings considered in the last chapter, Rembrandt also produced his most exciting etchings. The first of these, *Christ with the Sick,* is a fairly large work completed in 1649. It has become famous under the name *The Hundred-Guilder Print,* this being the price which it fetched at an auction *Ill. 95* shortly after its completion. There is even a theory that this was the amount which Rembrandt himself had to pay when one day he decided to buy back a good print of his etching.

Does the print deserve the fame which it enjoys? It is without question a remarkable work, and one which is in every way representative of Rembrandt's art as a whole. It reveals the interest with which Rembrandt regarded those who had little else but misfortunes and sufferings, and the contempt which he felt for the Pharisees, those hypocritical defenders of conventional values. It reveals his image of Christ—venerable but not solemn, gentle but not insipid. It also shows his particular brand of light, dazzling and subdued in turn, his downy shadows and velvety darkness. Finally, it displays his resourcefulness of draughtsmanship and freedom of style.

177

96 *The Flight into Egypt: A Night Piece.* 1651

In parts his line is as supple and slender as a hair, in others as sharp as a knife-edge. It is in turn both delicate and forceful. Things merely hinted at stand side by side with others which are strongly emphasized, suggestion alternates with explicit description. The entire group of Pharisees on the left of the print is hardly more than outlined. A vivid light strikes them, almost crushes them; it is as though Rembrandt wished to allow these men who doubted Christ only a doubtful existence themselves, as though he wished to overwhelm them with a light too brilliant to be withstood for long. The mothers and their children, the poor, the wretched and the sick are more firmly drawn. Their bodies are moulded by the shadow, and it is a warm light, not a harsh one, which falls upon them.

Thus in the same work Rembrandt did not hesitate to make use of two quite different styles. Moreover the fact that a character is

97 *The Triumph of Mordecai*. About 1650

situated in the foreground, like the old Jew with his back to us, does not automatically mean that he is portrayed in detail. The Jew is an almost completely blank outline, because, in the artist's view, this half-presence corresponded to his role in the composition. His cap, on the other hand, is drawn clearly enough to allow even the play of light on its dark material to be distinguished, no doubt because Rembrandt needed a dark patch at this point to provide a contrast. He displays the same freedom in his direction of light and his distribution of shade: both light and shade are really means which he places at the disposal of expression and the pictorial life of the work.

The smaller etching often called *La petite Tombe* (because it was published by the merchant Pieter de la Tombe) is more than a little similar to *The Hundred-Guilder Print*. Christ again stands facing the crowd, although this time he is preaching, not healing. Some of the people around him are listening humbly and trustingly, but others are simply curious onlookers, unwilling to be convinced right away. The variety in the attitudes and expressions confirms something which has already been frequently noted—Rembrandt observed his fellow-men closely, and whatever the setting in which he staged them, he took care that his characters should be realistically portrayed, human beings, not dull utility-actors. In this respect the work is in the same vein as *The Hundred-Guilder Print*.

Where it differs is in its style. The treatment is not so close and the arrangement more obvious. The curves and straight lines, and the relationships between them, are more clearly depicted than in the preceding work. The pattern of the curves no longer betrays the influence of baroque. They do not disturb the rhythm of the print. They are arcs which make the structure richer and in places more supple but which do not unsettle it.

Ill. 98 Chronologically situated between these two compositions is a far more simple print featuring only one small object, a *Shell* (1650). Despite its simplicity, it cannot be overlooked. The light is soft, the shadows are satiny, and altogether the work exudes a moving poetry. Although Rembrandt had included still-life objects in some of his youthful works and later on painted slaughtered animals, he had never produced pictures similar to those of Pieter Claesz or Willem Claesz Heda who managed to impart a secret, enthralling life to

180

98 *Shell.* 1650

objects such as glasses, pewter mugs, pipes, and snuff-boxes. By etching one of those shells such as Balthasar van der Ast featured in his work, Rembrandt demonstrated that he was also capable of handling an object of this kind with delicacy and sensitivity.

During this period Rembrandt also reverted to etching and drawing landscapes. These were usually views which he had actually seen, and he depicted them without the pathos of the *Three Trees* print. Nothing could be less artificial than *Trees near a Farm*, in which his very light but precise draughtsmanship simultaneously evokes the bright sunlight and the delightful cool shade cast by the leaves. No Dutch landscape could be more natural than *The Gold-Weigher's Field*, where the serene light and the fields stretching out across *Ill. 100* the plain combine to produce an impression of peacefulness. The mountains of his *Landscape with a Sportsman and Dogs* no doubt *Ill. 99* derived from his own imagination or from the work of another artist, but all its remaining features were probably drawn from life. These works breathe calm; they prove that Rembrandt sometimes drew his inspiration from a first-hand view of the outside world, just as much in order to rest his mind as to enrich it. The few landscapes which still appeared in his paintings in the early 1650s are less romantic and closer to Dutch scenery than in previous works.

Ills 101, 102   The landscape in *St Jerome*, however, whom Rembrandt portrayed in both etching and drawing about 1653, is quite different. This setting was provided not by the Dutch countryside but by Italian painting, for the hill and buildings in the background seem to be ideas borrowed from Titian. Sir Kenneth Clark remarks that the positioning of St Jerome in luxuriant natural surroundings rather than in a desert also betrays Venetian influence, since the first artist

99 *Landscape with a Sportsman and Dogs.* About 1653

100 *The Gold-Weigher's Field.* 1651

to adopt such an approach was Giovanni Bellini. Yet, once again, Rembrandt preserves his individuality; his use of realism, in particular, displays a freedom which his Italian predecessors never knew and which they would not, indeed, have regarded as desirable.

While, in the etching, the buildings in the distance are drawn fairly precisely, the saint in the foreground is only a vague outline. Physically, St Jerome has less reality than his surroundings. Is this because he is so absorbed in the Bible that he is no longer conscious of his physical existence and has become estranged from the surrounding world? Or is it that the artist needed a bright patch at that particular point to correspond to the light hill, and at the same time to contrast with the thick shadows behind the saint? Rembrandt was probably influenced by both considerations.

There is less chiaroscuro in the drawing, but line plays a more important part. It has all the characteristics of a rough sketch—spirited, hasty, in places vague, it is at other points most evocative and concise. The lion in the drawing, for instance, looks far more lifelike than its counterpart in the etching, although it is filled out in less detail.

It has been seen how easily Rembrandt, in his paintings, could transfer from a biblical theme to *Aristotle* or *The Polish Rider*. Likewise, he was capable of passing, in his etchings, from *St Jerome* to *Faust in his Study* (or rather the opposite, since *Faust* is a slightly older work than the other). *Faust* is another example of a character

Ill. 103

183

101 *St Jerome in a Landscape*. About 1653

Ill. 80 in a room full of deep shadows. It is interesting to compare this work with *Jan Six reading*, where the setting is similar. The two prints are separated by about five years and also, of course, by the fact that *Jan Six* is a portrait, while *Faust* is entirely a product of

102 *St Jerome in a Landscape.* About 1653

the artist's imagination. The objects in the latter work are far less realistic than in the other, and can be identified only with difficulty. The important thing is no longer their substance, hardly even their shape, but the different kinds of light which brush their surface. Even

103 *Faust in his Study.* About 1653

more than in the etching of 1647, the central character is really the light, the light of an apparition which substitutes its sharp, fascinating brilliance for the peaceful daylight of the world outside.

In *Jan Six* there is, on the one hand, a reader concentrating on his book and, on the other, objects of which this reader is not conscious but which have an independent existence of their own. The objects which surround Faust, by contrast, exist only in so far as the glare emanating from the cabbalistic signs has not completely effaced them from the scene. Rembrandt here reduces the role of accessories to a minimum in order to concentrate attention on the main thing, which is the light and its many varieties. The origin of this light is, of course, the white of the paper, which is basically the same white as in the window, the radiant disk and the doctor's cap. Yet the black lines give it a variety of appearances—restrained, vivid, sparkling.

If this print displays several kinds of light, *The Adoration of the Shepherds* displays several kinds of darkness. Although the subject *Ill. 105* lent itself to this treatment, in none of his previous versions had Rembrandt granted such an important position to darkness. In the two paintings of 1646 the characters are immediately distinguishable; the night surrounds, but does not engulf, them. Here, in contrast, the darkness is so powerful that the bodies melt into it and the faces are only barely visible. The Child is no more than a frail patch of white shrouded in dark greys. The Virgin, who is watching him anxiously, seems to huddle into a haycock, a small, pale figure assailed by the blackness. St Joseph is even more dimly illuminated, although a bright but restricted light strikes the pages of the book which he holds in his hand. This light emanates from the lantern carried by one of the shepherds in the middle of the print; its two small rectangles are the brightest part of the whole work.

Everything is thus brought out only by suggestion, but the attitude and expression of the Virgin have immense eloquence. How expressive are the ghostlike faces of the shepherds! It is doubtful whether the surprise, curiosity and awe of these simple men have ever been rendered with such an evocative economy of means. What other artist, moreover, has managed to convey so well what it meant for the Virgin to have to seek refuge in a stable, and give birth to a child in the cold of the night? Rembrandt's biblical characters are not people whom the speculations of theologians and the devotion of the

104 *The Adoration of the Shepherds.* About 1654

faithful have removed from the world of ordinary mortals. For him they were kindred spirits with whom he shared his joys and sorrows. Yet he did not diminish them in stature or bring them down to the level of the commonplace. He portrayed them with familiarity, but also with fervour and that religiousness which, far from being dictated to him by a church, was naturally linked to his view of life.

Certain of Rembrandt's etchings exist in a number of states, and the difference between first and last is sometimes considerable. In *The Three Crosses* the divergence between the first version and the last is so great that the very meaning of the work is modified.

Ills 106, 107

The Three Crosses is a rather large-scale work (it measures no less than 38.7×45 cm) showing not only the crucifixion of Christ but also that of the two thieves, together with a crowd of participants and onlookers. Rembrandt's first attempt at the subject is determinedly narrative in style, although he avoids detailed description— the year of its execution was 1653, and at this late stage of his career he normally expressed a great deal in a few lines.

188

The pale body of Christ stands out against a slightly darkened background, over which pours a torrent of light, steady but already threatened by the gloom. The light crashes down on the unrepentant thief, who meets it stiffly with his stubborn refusal to yield. The Virgin and Christ's disciples are also covered in a light so bright that their bodies are totally lacking in depth and seem to be consumed by grief. In the foreground are the grey forms of two Jews hurrying away from the scene (one of them has been interpreted as Joseph of Arimathea going to Pilate to plead for the body of Christ, which he wishes to bury). Minor detail also appears in the form of a frightened dog whose barking seems to startle the two men. In addition there are Roman soldiers, one of whom has dismounted from his horse and kneels before the cross, some women in tears, and other Jews disturbed by the sinister light and the implacable darkness which is about to overwhelm it.

105 *The Adoration of the Shepherds: a Night Piece.* 1652

106 *The Three Crosses. 1653*

Ill. 107   In the fourth state the whole of this group has vanished. One of the two Jews in the foreground has also disappeared, while his colleague is no more than a dark, shapeless mass. The bad thief has rejected the light and is now plunged into darkness. The Virgin and the disciples are also sunk in blackness; only a few patches of wan light evoke their faces, as though on this occasion Rembrandt was trying to express the struggle of their thoughts to emerge from their crushing grief. Christ stands out better than in the earlier state, due to the darker background. The light, which is hemmed in on all sides

190

107 *The Three Crosses.* 1653

by darkness, seems to take refuge in him; it shimmers like a bright
flame putting up a lone resistance to the night.

There are other significant changes. The kneeling soldier is now
hardly brought out at all, whereas another soldier who did not
appear in the first state immediately catches the attention. He sits
bolt upright on his horse, with a profile derived from a Pisanello
medal and a peculiar hat, a very odd figure in the context of the
work. Two possible explanations for the introduction of this character spring to mind. He may be intended to represent the rigid,

108 *The Presentation in the Temple.* 1654

impassive guardian of the law, executing all orders, even the cruellest, with indifference, and detached from the event which he witnesses. On the other hand, Rembrandt may have inserted him simply because he had recently seen the Pisanello medal, found it impressive, and wished to make use of it in his work.

Behind the rider is a rearing horse. The movement of this animal is nobler than that of the barking dog, and is also an effective way of showing that it is not only the people present who are terror-stricken. For this, in the last resort, is the characteristic feature of the final state of *The Three Crosses*. The drama exceeds the world of men, it concerns the entire universe. The forces of light do battle with the forces of darkness in a pathetic, harrowing conflict.

When one comes to consider what Rembrandt put in the place of the omitted characters and how he managed to broaden and deepen the meaning of the work, the answer is simply lines, greys, whites, and patches of black—in other words, the means of modern abstract art. At some points the lines are scribbled impetuously, at others drawn with a ruler. In places his strokes leave the white paper a doubtful, languid and contorted existence, while elsewhere they tear through it or blot it out with finality. The blacks are thick in parts but not opaque, so that the eye is not halted on the surface of the paper. On the contrary, it penetrates into a vast world full of cold and gloom, tensions, agitation and anguish.

For Rembrandt to have proceeded further along this path would have required a total abandonment of figuration. In the period when he worked this was obviously out of the question, especially as his basic aim was to create not only shapes but scenes. From now on, however, his scenes tended to become simpler and more concentrated, with all but the indispensable elements discarded.

This point is well illustrated by the *Presentation in the Temple*   *Ill. 108*
which he etched about 1654. Compared with this print even the painted version of 1631 appears distinctly anecdotal. Here, the fundamental unimportance of all the people in the temple, who are mere gaping onlookers, and the architectural details is revealed. Now only a few characters enact the scene and the architecture is evoked only sparingly, yet the meaning of the episode stands out quite clearly. The Virgin and St Joseph, who, according to the Bible, do not properly understand what is going on, are abandoned to shadow

109 *The Descent from the Cross.* 1654

in order that the attention may immediately focus on Simeon and the Child whom he holds in his arms. The light is distributed in such a way that the eye moves naturally on from Simeon to the High Priest, and finally to the majestic figure of the old man who stands slightly set back from the others with a torch in his hand. If it is difficult to identify this, the tallest of the characters, the reason for his presence can easily be discerned: his function is to heighten the solemn, hieratic atmosphere of the scene and to enrich the print with a mysterious, sparkling light. This accounts not only for the torch but also the sumptuousness of his clothing and that of the High Priest.

After the fourth state of *The Three Crosses* Rembrandt, not surprisingly, ceased to attach the same importance to conveying the opulence and weight of fabrics. His aim in doing so here was not, as formerly, to produce tactile sensations on the part of the onlooker, but to render the spiritual significance of the scene more effectively. He succeeded in conjuring up all the pomp of an official church, together with the self-effacement and humility of those who attend religious ceremonies: this he achieved through the play of light and shade and, more particularly, through a dignified arrangement. Geometrical shapes, especially angles and triangles, can easily be detected, while the character in the background suggests long, imposing verticals. The vertical line running down from his torch meets the horizontal of the throne on which the High Priest is seated, and together the two lines form almost a full right angle, which contains the heads of Simeon and the Child.

Structure, emphasized by light, is no less eloquent in Rembrandt's *Descent from the Cross* of 1654. The sheet being used to lower the *Ill. 109* body of Christ marks a strong diagonal, which the edge of the bank carries on right down to the litter below. Placed sideways, and parallel to the body which it is about to receive, this litter is covered by a shroud, whose rather calm whiteness contrasts with the bright, dramatic, painful white of the sheet. Beneath the head of Christ stands a man whose outstretched hand breaches the darkness like a torch, and who links the upper group to the characters below. The eye would be forced down too abruptly, however, but for the architectural mass above which breaks its fall. This building performs two further functions; it gives an impression of space at a point which would otherwise be merely a screen of darkness, and it intro-

Christ presented to the People. 1655

duces the monumental stability of right angles to an etching whose essential means of expression is asymmetrical curved lines.

There are other works, however, in which the right angle plays a far more important part. One of these is an *Entombment* after a drawing by an Italian artist with affinities to Raphael. The fact that Rembrandt should have wished to copy such a work and, furthermore, should have preserved the grouping, with all its stiff symmetry, intact, is even more interesting than the actual drawing which he produced. This was another instance of Rembrandt doing homage

to the classicism which had haunted him for so long. He again
showed a concern, which was to recur later on, to annex styles
which, though serving a useful purpose as a corrective, were basically alien to his own artistic nature. The firm bone-structure in
his own version of *The Entombment*, which he etched about 1654,   *Ill. 112*
shows unmistakable similarities with the Italian work, despite his
rejection of its clarity of structure, ballet-like movements, and
impassive light. Even in the second state, where there is a strong
tendency for chiaroscuro to undermine linear construction, an ellipse
is suggested by the arch of the tomb and the disposition of the

111 *Christ presented to the People.* 1655

characters, while, inside this ellipse, vertical and horizontal lines form rectangles which, for all their unobtrusiveness, are active elements in the structure.

Nowhere, however, are right angles, rectangles, and segments of a circle more important or conspicuous in Rembrandt's work than in *Christ presented to the People* (1655), an etching which in size and beauty is comparable to *The Three Crosses,* although far removed in spirit. The original inspiration for this work probably came from an engraving by Lucas van Leyden; as in van Leyden's version of 1510 Rembrandt positioned Christ on a podium, and in the early states of his composition he similarly portrayed an animated crowd in front of it. Rembrandt also owed to his predecessor certain details of his architecture. The rigorous construction, its relationship with the characters, and the tendency to symmetry, on the other hand, seem to reflect another influence, an engraving by Marcantonio after Bandinelli's *Martyrdom of St Lawrence.* In Sir Kenneth Clark's opinion, yet a third source should be added, an engraving by Antonio da Salamanca which reproduces Michelangelo's *Monument to Julius II.* It is a plausible theory, since the most prominent characteristics of this etching—the sharp contrast between verticals and horizontals, and the division of the architectural features into rectangles with the sculptures enclosed in a rigid framework—can also be found in Rembrandt's print. Nevertheless, here as elsewhere, Rembrandt differs from all the artists on whom he may have modelled himself. His narrative is far more pungent than Lucas van Leyden's; his architecture lacks the pseudo-antiquity of Bandinelli's; his characters have neither the studied bearing of actors on a stage nor the heroic look of Michelangelo's statues.

Seven states of this print are known to us. In all of the first four Rembrandt includes a watching, shouting, gesticulating crowd in front of the podium where Pilate is presenting Christ. Needless to say, the role of these characters is of considerable importance: they form part of the throng which has later to choose between Jesus and Barabbas, and whose clamouring determines the governor's decision. Yet in the last three states Rembrandt completely omits them, leaving in their place only the bare base of the podium. The apparent reason for this is that Rembrandt thought their presence prevented Christ from immediately capturing the attention.

At this point of his career, as has already been seen, Rembrandt invariably finished up by concentrating on the main point. In order to make this stand out strongly, he was quite prepared to prune his composition, even to dispense with things which he had originally considered important and which, for a mere narrative artist, would have remained so. But the role of narrative in his works was exactly what Rembrandt was now tending to reduce. While he did not carry abstraction to such lengths as in the fourth state of *The Three Crosses*, he still changed this etching in the same direction. One might say that he replaced the epic style by the dramatic. At any rate, he concentrates the action, marks off the different groups more clearly, and draws them more firmly; to compensate for the disappearance of the characters in front of the podium he makes the crowd on the left denser.

He also alters the base of the podium. Firstly he removes the strip of ground on which it formerly stood, thereby bringing it, and at the same time Christ and the people around him, closer to the front. Secondly he cuts into it two rounded openings, which lead to an underground chasm of impenetrable darkness. This has been interpreted as the mouth of a drain or a cesspool. But perhaps there is no need to look for any symbolic significance. As with other shapes in Rembrandt's work, these openings may be explicable purely in terms of plastic requirements. It was quite normal that Rembrandt should not have been satisfied with a bare wall. He probably thought this great empty surface would lack interest, and therefore introduced grey and black to offset the white of the podium's facing, just as he had to contrast two curves with the long horizontal of its upper edge. Since these curves could only be inserted in an architectural framework, nothing could be more natural than to make them into stone arches, especially as he may, as Sir Kenneth Clark thinks, have had the arches of the etching after Bandinelli in mind.

Between the arches Rembrandt placed a kind of mask. Sir Kenneth sees in this a link with Michelangelo, and indeed it is a Michelangelesque feature. Possibly its purpose was to evoke the presence of Rome in a work where a Roman official plays such a decisive part. One thing at any rate is certain. Whereas in the sixth state of this print the character on the mask can be clearly seen supporting his bearded chin on his right hand, in the seventh he is partially obscured

112 *The Entombment.* 1654

by the shadow and only barely visible; in the end he is less important than the light and darkness which clash in him. Another respect in which the last state differs from the rest, and more especially from the first four, is in its appreciably more expressive lighting. While in the early states almost the whole scene is covered with the same even light, with the exception of a few shallow shadows, in the final state Rembrandt establishes such strong tensions between bright light and deep darkness that this simple contrast alone reveals that the work is a treatment of dramatic events.

The clear and strictly ordered composition of this etching has no parallel in Rembrandt's painting. This discrepancy can be explained by the difference in the medium. The lines which can be drawn with a brush are different from lines drawn by an etching-needle on metal. Besides, Rembrandt expressed himself in his paintings less through brush strokes than through clusters of colour. Finally, he liked the sensual aspect of colour, and as time went by he set greater and greater store by pictorial content.

Rembrandt's desire to study styles alien to his own has already been noted in considering *The Entombment*, which reproduced an Italian drawing. This concern displayed itself in even more unexpected form when, between 1652 and 1656, he executed some twenty drawings after Indian miniatures. A great number of these miniatures have been traced; during the 18th century certain of them featured in the Habsburg collection in Vienna, and Maria Theresa used some to decorate the 'Hall of the millions' in Schloss Schönbrunn. How did Rembrandt react to the miniatures, which were so different from his own work in their exoticism, their delicacy, and the slenderness of their characters? In fact, although he set himself to copying them with very light draughtsmanship, he also allowed himself to make certain 'improvements' in order to bring them closer to his own art. His drawing of the old men in *The Emperor Akbar enthroned*, for *Ill. 113* instance, gives them more moral presence as well as more physical poise.

113 *The Emperor Akbar enthroned.* 1650–56

CHAPTER SEVENTEEN

Ruin

The written documents which inform us about Rembrandt's career frequently reveal unpleasant, distressing details. How often they speak of wills, burials, trials, loans, acknowledgments of debts, and securities! In the 1650s in particular, financial matters crop up with a regularity which it would take an accountant or a notary to appreciate.

On one occasion in 1653 Rembrandt obtained a loan of 4180 guilders from the former deputy-mayor of Amsterdam, Cornelis Witsen. He promised to repay the sum in a year's time, pledging his entire belongings as security. On another occasion Christoffel Thijssens, the former owner of his house, presented the artist with a bill for the balance due on the property he had bought in 1639, according to which Rembrandt had not yet paid half what he owed. It will be recalled that the selling price of the house was 13,000 guilders, and that Rembrandt had undertaken to pay off this amount in full within five or six years. For three and a half years, however, he had not even paid the interest, and the total figure that Thijssens claimed from him was 8470 guilders.

It therefore comes as no surprise that Rembrandt, having just borrowed money from Witsen, had to borrow some more, still in

1653, from Jan Six and Isaac van Hertsbeeck. To Hertsbeeck, from whom he received 4200 guilders, he made the same promise as he had to Witsen: the entire sum was to be paid back in a year's time, and his goods were pledged as security. He pledged them once again in 1654, in a declaration acknowledging that he owed Christoffel Thijssens an annual amount of just over 52 guilders, a debt which he could alternatively discharge outright by a payment of 1168 guilders plus interest.

In the meantime, Rembrandt had given instructions for the money that was due to him to be collected. He sought to obtain payment of a draft for 1005 guilders, plus an additional 40 guilders interest. While this was perfectly understandable, another demand which he made in 1656 was less so, indeed it was disturbing—that Geertghe Dircx's brother should repay him the 140 guilders which he had advanced a few years before, at the time when Geertghe was confined to a mental hospital. Rembrandt went further; when the brother refused to pay up, he had him thrown into prison. The documents do not reveal the undercurrents of this affair; it may be that Geertghe's brother was rude or exasperating to Rembrandt. But, in any case, the fact that the artist thought it necessary to recover such a meagre sum by such means, and remained unyielding when the man, who wished to take service as a carpenter on a ship, asked to be released, and even decided to bring an action against him, shows that his own financial position cannot have been at all healthy.

Indeed, it was not. Rembrandt had over-indulged his liking for collecting, without giving a thought to the possible consequences. He had also been too insistent on following only his own inclinations in painting. His bold style, his heavy impasto, his almost complete disregard for anecdote, the liberties which he took with realism, all this was far from corresponding to contemporary taste and eventually caused clients to turn away from him. Moreover, the pupils he had trained offered certain of his special characteristics, while at the same time rejecting his excesses, so that the public was able to find in them the qualities which it had once appreciated in Rembrandt. This is a common phenomenon; the genius of the master is disconcerting, but the talent of his disciples reassuring, particularly when, instead of producing startling new works, they regurgitate their instructor's original discoveries in more palatable form.

On 17 May 1656, Rembrandt declared to the Chamber of Orphans that his house in the Breestraat was to be registered in the name of his son, as forming part of the inheritance which Titus had received from Saskia. It is easy to understand the reasons behind this step; Rembrandt's creditors were becoming impatient and, realizing that his fortune was in danger, the artist was trying to safeguard the house which, only a short while before, he had given so readily as security to those who lent him money. All this achieved was to make his creditors even more uneasy, and to make them press even harder for their money. As a result, a few weeks later Rembrandt could see no other way out of his predicament than to ask the town council of Amsterdam to declare him insolvent. By way of explanation for his request, he said he had 'suffered losses in trade and at sea', a phrase which, according to some, was merely a formula, but which has led others to say, without producing any evidence, that Rembrandt had bought ships which were wrecked at sea. One thing we know for certain: on 20 July a receiver was appointed, and charged with instituting the liquidation of all the artist's belongings. We also have in our possession the inventory of Rembrandt's property drawn up on 25 and 26 July, which enables us to know exactly what he had accumulated in his house.

We have seen that his two favourite artists were Adriaen Brouwer and Hercules Seghers. He owned seven pictures by the first, and eight by the second. In addition, he possessed nine paintings by Jan Lievens, his former colleague, and two by Pieter Lastman, his former instructor. He also had a *Head of the Virgin*, two *Little Dogs*, and a '*geschilderd boek*' (a book with water-colours?) by his son Titus, who had been a pupil of his. Other Dutch artists were represented: Jan Porcellis, the seascape-painter, by five works; Aert van Leyden by three; Jan Pynas and Govert Jansz by two; Lucas van Leyden, Hendrick Anthonisz, Simon de Vlieger, and the young Hals (a brother or son of Frans) by one picture each. Although the collection no longer included Rubens' *Hero and Leander*, which Rembrandt had resold in 1644, it did contain a *Head of an old Man* by van Eyck, a *Small Winter Landscape* by Abel Grimmer, and two *Small Heads* by Lucas van Valckenburgh.

Besides these works by Dutch and Flemish artists there were several examples of Italian painting: a *Head* and *Virgin* by Raphael, which have already been encountered, a composition by Bassano, a *Crucifixion* by Lelio Orsi da Novellara, and two copies after works by Annibale Carracci. The inventory also lists Giorgione's *Samaritan Woman* and Palma Vecchio's *Rich Man*, but these were works of which Rembrandt owned only a half share, the co-owner being the merchant Pieter de la Tombe who had given his name to the etching of Christ preaching.

The etchings which the house in the Breestraat contained were greater in number, including original creations as well as reproductions. The inventory records the special value of the etchings by Mantegna and those executed after Raphael, but merely enumerates the rest. Notable names which figure in the list are Vanni, Baroccio, Antonio Tempesta, Annibale, Agostino and Ludovico Carracci, Guido Reni, Spagnoletto, Titian and Michelangelo, of the Italians; Cranach, Melchior Lorch, Schongauer and Holbein, of the Germans; Bruegel the Elder, Rubens, van Dyck, Jordaens, Cock and Frans Floris, of the Flemings; Lucas van Leyden, Goltzius, Heemskerck, Mierevelt, Buytewech, Bloemaert, Lastman, Lievens, Ferdinand Bol and van Vliet, of the Dutch painters.

Elsewhere we learn that Rembrandt possessed a work (or cartoon) with *erotica* by Raphael, Rosso, Annibale Carracci, and Giulio Bonasone; Dürer's four books on proportion; drawings by Brouwer, Jacques Callot and Roland Savery; other drawings executed by the 'leading masters in the world'; 'a book with landscapes by various masters' etc. If the majority of the etchings were bought for their artistic qualities, there were others which were probably acquired principally for the information which they brought Rembrandt about the outside world: they showed views and buildings in Rome, Turkish buildings and scenes from Turkish life, and statues and architecture of indeterminate origin. Thus Rembrandt, who never left his native land, must have travelled far in mind, both in time and space.

His sculptures also allowed him to escape from his own period and environment. They include a small *Head* by Michelangelo and also portraits of the German sculptor-etcher Barthel Beham and his wife, but in the main the sculptures in the collection are of ancient origin. A *Sybil*, a *Laocoon* and various anonymous heads and statues feature alongside busts of Homer, Heraclitus, Socrates, Aristotle and—very surprisingly—busts and statues of Roman emperors: Julius Ceasar, Augustus, Tiberius, Caligula, Nero, Galba, Otho, Vitellius, Vespasian, Titus, Domitian and Aurelian.

We have already seen that Rembrandt's curiosity was not limited to painting, sculpture and prints, that he had bought medals, glasses, porcelain and fans. He had also bought pieces of coral, shells, minerals, 'land and sea creatures', stag's horns, globes, Spanish chairs, Indian robes, a death mask of Prince Maurice of Orange, casts from human hands, arms, heads (among them the head of a Negro) etc. In addition to this, the inventory lists seven stringed instruments, a harp, bamboo wind instruments, flutes, a wooden trumpet, and numerous weapons—halberds, bows, arrows, a cross-bow, assegais, swords, a small cannon, a pistol, cuirasses, shields and helmets. One of these helmets had been made to fit a giant: another was Japanese, while one of the bows was Turkish and a powder-horn East Indian.

One item which, in contrast, was a rarity in the artist's house was literary works. At one point 'fifteen books of various sizes' are recorded, but no more specific information given. Five other books are also mentioned; of these three are written in German, so presumably they were bought for their illustrations. The fourth work is Jan Six's tragedy *Medea* for which, it will be recalled, Rembrandt had made an engraving. The fifth is an 'old Bible'. From this it is reasonable to assume that, for Rembrandt, the Bible was the book of books, and that he had little inclination to read anything else.

The inventory also, of course, includes his own works—almost seventy paintings, many etchings, and a very large number of drawings. Even the linen in the wash-house is recorded: three men's shirts, six handkerchiefs, twelve towels, three tablecloths, and some collars and cuffs.

When all the items had been carefully inscribed on the lists, Rembrandt could do no more than await the sale. A sale was even more imperative in the eyes of his creditors in that the men already mentioned were not the only ones to whom he owed money. In September, three others appeared on the scene (they were not the last). One of them claimed 848 guilders, the second 1605, and the third a sum so substantial that Rembrandt was forced to undertake to hand over some paintings in the event that the proceeds from the sale were insufficient to settle the whole debt.

A first sale was organized in December 1657, at the Keyserskroon hotel in the Kalverstraat, at which Rembrandt's paintings and certain objets d'art were on offer. At the second auction, which took place in February 1658, his house and furniture were sold, and at the last one, held in September 1658, his drawings and etchings. All these sales dragged on, and the money they realized was ridiculously little.

In June 1657, a series of paintings forming part of the inheritance of the art dealer Johannes de Renialme had been valued in Amsterdam. Among them were twelve works by Rembrandt, whose value was assessed at 2568 guilders; one picture alone, *The Woman taken in Adultery* of 1644, was estimated at 1500 guilders. In the sale of Rembrandt's possessions there were not only almost six times as many pictures but also hundreds of drawings, etchings, objets d'art, and collectors' items. Yet, when the proceeds of the sale came to be calculated, it emerged that, even including the price obtained for the house (11,218 guilders), there was not enough money to pay off the 20,000 guilders or so which were due to creditors. Despite the fact that he had been stripped of all his possessions, Rembrandt was still insolvent. He was to remain so until he died.

This was a situation which he cannot of course have regarded without revulsion and bitterness. No man can be deprived of his passionately assembled belongings without feeling sad at heart. Moreover, Rembrandt not only saw his house emptied of all its contents, he was also obliged to get used to the idea that the house itself would have to be vacated. He did not, however, move out immediately. He seems not to have left until around the end of 1660, which was when the property was paid for by its new owner. For three and a half years, therefore, he lived in a temporary state; he experienced worries and humiliations, and was compelled to allow others to interfere in his own affairs and to call him to account. Troubles even arose when the Chamber of Orphans appointed a new guardian for Titus. In an effort to protect the interests of the child to the best of his ability, the new guardian insisted on obtaining all kinds of certificates intended to establish Titus' share in Saskia's inheritance.

One of the documents certifies that this inheritance amounted to 40,750 guilders. Further certificates reveal that, after his wife's death, Rembrandt had in his possession two large pearl necklaces and

Ill. 114

114 *The Woman taken in Adultery.* 1644

some jewels, and another that he sold one of these necklaces to the painter Philips Koninck. Yet others mention the prices which he had received for some of his paintings: in 1647, 1,600 guilders for a *Susanna;* in 1642, 500 guilders for a portrait. Roughly the same price (530 guilders) was paid to him in 1644 for Rubens' *Hero and Leander.* We also learn on this occasion how much *The Night Watch* brought him—1,600 guilders. Further, a certificate by two art dealers discloses that between 1640 and 1650 Rembrandt's collection was worth at least 17,100 guilders, 6,400 of which represented the value of the pictures. The obvious effect, if not aim, of all this was to establish that at one time Rembrandt had been well off, that a lot of money had passed through his hands, and that he had made extremely poor use of it.

One can imagine the disapproving looks which were cast in his direction, and the disparaging remarks which were made behind his back. This man had thought he could live according to his own rules; now society was calling him to order. There can be no doubt that his fellow-citizens were pleased with this opportunity for taking their revenge, especially as Rembrandt's insolvency was not the only source of irritation; his individualistic religious conceptions and morality also gave cause for offence. Finally, they must have been antagonized by the artist's show of independence, and the obstinacy with which he preferred to satisfy his own requirements rather than the public taste.

CHAPTER EIGHTEEN

Refusal to surrender

Rembrandt carried on working during these years, and his art reveals something about the way in which he bore these blows. Between 1657 and 1660 he produced some ten self-portraits, more than he had ever painted in such a short period, except at the beginning of his career. It is as though, in the face of adversity, he felt the need to assert himself more, and to subject himself to a searching self-examination. At any rate, these portraits reveal not a broken man but a man whom events have failed to undermine. The body remains sturdy and the face broad. Of course, the trials he had endured left some mark. The brow is battered and furrowed by deep wrinkles, the expression is sometimes very tense, and occasionally a stormy light flickers on the cheeks and around the mouth. But the gaze remains steady, not averted from the onlooker's but holding it, even if possibly by an effort of will.

Rembrandt might have been deprived of his entire belongings, but this did not prevent him from painting himself with the air of a monarch, firmly ensconced in his chair as though granting an

115 *Self-portrait.* 1660

116 *David harping before Saul.* About 1657

audience. Yet lordly as his clothes may be in the *Self-Portrait* (1658) of the Frick Collection, New York, it is no longer elegance which the painter is seeking, but a sumptuousness which will impress others, and demonstrate his dignity and social position. The effect of the clothing is heightened by the frontal presentation, which makes the massive body most imposing and gives great authority to the face. There is not a trace of weariness in the features; on the contrary, they express a determination not to surrender.

Certain slightly later works, however, reveal that Rembrandt was here making up a face which, basically, was no longer a true likeness.

He did so because he was involved in a struggle and he did not wish his opponents to think that spiritually he felt a ruined man. In this portrait, in other words, he was still paying attention to his enemies and to public opinion. Before long, he ceased to care whether the picture which people had of him was true or false, and attached importance only to the truth which he himself could detect in his features.

Ill. 115 The *Self-Portrait* in the Louvre (1660) leaves no room for doubt on this point. One can no longer perceive any concern to present a favourable image of himself. He wears no disguise; he makes not the slightest attempt to break away from his real nature and his profession. He is a painter, and he portrays himself at his easel, palette and brushes in hand. Although he still wears a dressing-gown (or coat) with a fur-trimmed collar, this time it is a threadbare garment, with nothing stylish about it, which he no doubt liked because of the various lighting effects it allowed him to bring into play. The velvet beret which he once wore so often (and which he was to wear again) has given way to a plain white cap. The flesh of the face is flaccid, the cheeks ill-shaven, and the eyes full of that tenacious seriousness imparted by continued setbacks. The carelessness which has crept into his appearance should be interpreted as a refusal to take the tastes of others into consideration. Rembrandt is here a lonely man who accepts solitude because it allows him to be completely honest with himself.

In any case, his solitude was not total. There was always the comforting presence of Hendrickje, Titus, and Cornelia; perhaps he even found that this was enough. During this period he once again used Hendrickje as a model on several occasions. In one picture *Ill. 117* (c. 1657) he painted her as *Flora,* as he had Saskia in the past. But he did not adorn her with as many flowers as his first wife in 1634; he did not give her a sumptuous dress to wear; he did not reduce her face to that of a doll. The portrait is a rather flattering one, but he does not fail to bring out her natural goodness and gentleness. With her presentation in profile and the large hat she is wearing, Hendrickje is even more reminiscent of the *Saskia* of the Gemäldegalerie, *Ill. 29* Kassel, than *Saskia as Flora* in the Hermitage, Leningrad. But the colouring of this new work is more restrained, and the body no longer cuts sideways through space—it spreads across the full width

214

of the canvas, thus preserving its evenness. The triangle described by the outline of body and arms adds clarity to stability.

Hendrickje once more gave her features to a mythological character, or rather reappeared herself, in a work entitled *Venus and Cupid*, Cupid's face being that of her daughter Cornelia. In actual fact, only the small wings on the child are at all evocative of a mythological subject. One would never dream of seeing the goddess of love in this woman whose broad, podgy face and body seem to lack any carnal attraction. In fact, the body is not even visible, being covered by a heavy dress, whereas in the normal way a painter portraying Venus would take pleasure in displaying an attractive naked body.

How is one to interpret this picture? Was Rembrandt once again reacting against classicism and the fashion for idealization? Was he trying to substitute truth for falsehood, two real human beings for imaginary creatures? Did he wish to contrast affection with sensuality, tenderness with physical love? Or did he simply set out to paint a double portrait and only invent this title when the picture was practically completed, because he thought he needed to make the pyramidal structure of the composition slightly less severe by including a few light patches behind the little girl, which might be justified by wings? Here again, it is safe to assume that a variety of reasons influenced him; even if Rembrandt did not start off with the intention of adopting an anti-classical attitude, he certainly wished it to be understood that for him the world of men with its humble everyday reality was more important than the adventures and splendours of ancient gods.

Moreover, the most moving portraits of Hendrickje are those in which all reference to mythology is avoided. If she sometimes wears more jewels and is dressed more deliberately than in previous portraits, this is probably because Rembrandt wished to adorn her in things which, in the eyes of the world, she ought no longer to possess. Although all these works were painted in the same period (c. 1659–60), Hendrickje's age in them seems to vary, but her expression always reveals the same loyalty. In the painting of 1660 in the Metropolitan Museum, New York, she is leaning slightly forward with a sad look on her face; her eyes seem to be clouded with worried thoughts; she gives an impression of suffering. But perhaps Rembrandt wished to do no more than record the tender way in which she looked at her

117 *Hendrickje as Flora.* 1657

daughter Cornelia: her attitude, indeed, is that of a Virgin contemplating the Child.

Titus also posed for his father on several further occasions. A portrait of 1655 showed him facing full-on, with a pen in his hand *Ill. 89* and a searching gaze directed not so much at the onlooker but rather at life and its complexities. In a work executed around 1657, on the *Ill. 118* other hand, he appears at a three-quarters angle, his eyes lowered on a book which commands the whole of his attention. His face is covered in soft shadow interspersed with a few patches of light. Far from making the features sharp, light and shade combine to make them blurred and the model more distant. He is completely unconscious of the ordinary world, which he has left for a world of fiction from which we remain excluded. Even the mouth is rather indistinct: it has almost ceased to be a normal mouth and become instead a kind of sensitive membrane on which the words of the book register just as strongly as on the retina. Even more strikingly than in *Jan Six* Rembrandt here renders that half-absence, half-presence which characterizes the reader engrossed in his text.

However, the serene brightness of Titus' face in this picture is an exception. In the portrait in the Louvre (c. 1657) it looks almost sickly, and his gaze is astonishingly serious for a young man of 18. It may have been his father's anxiety which gave him this appearance, but it was probably also his genuine state of health. No doubt it was both: Titus was the only one of Saskia's children not to die at a very early age, and Rembrandt must always have felt that he was menaced by the same fate. He loved his son and had good reason to, for Titus' behaviour towards his father was admirable.

At the age of 16 he had gone to a notary and made a will by which his half-sister Cornelia became his residuary legatee, while his father and Hendrickje were to be her guardians and Rembrandt was to hold the inheritance in usufruct for the duration of his life. Other stipulations of the will specified that Rembrandt's revenues were to be used only for his own keep and not for paying off debts, that there would be no need for him to draw up an inventory, and that he was not to allow any third party to intervene in the question of the legacy.

On 15 December 1660 Titus, assisted by his father and accompanied by Hendrickje, again went to see a notary. This time it was to register an agreement which they had reached, and whose essential

217

terms were as follows. For more than two years, Hendrickje and Titus had been running an art business, selling paintings, drawings, engravings, woodcuts, curios etc., and also making prints of etchings. They now decided to continue this business until six years after Rembrandt's death, under the following conditions: as hitherto, they were to share the costs of the housekeeping and all related expenses; they had paid jointly for furniture, objets d'art, curios and rent and taxes, and would do so in the future. They had given the company all they possessed (Titus, more especially, had contributed his presents, savings, and earnings), and they were to continue to give it everything they might subsequently acquire. Each was to receive half the profits, and bear half the losses.

Since in their art business they needed an assistant, and nobody would be better able to help them than Rembrandt, they had agreed that he should live in their house and receive board and lodging, on condition that he help them in every possible way. But he was to take no share in the business or the housekeeping, and the contracting parties were to remain the perpetual owners of all the collections and objects in their house. Anything that Rembrandt might earn would also belong to the business. As he had just gone bankrupt and had had to part with his entire possessions, the partners had been obliged to support him, and he acknowledged receipt of 950 guilders from Titus and 800 from Hendrickje, which he was to repay as soon as his painting brought him in some more money. By way of guaranteeing this promise, he was to assign to Titus and Hendrickje all the pictures which he painted in their house, or the amount which he eventually received for them.

One need not be a great enthusiast of legal documents to delve into this particular one with interest, and indeed excitement. Its bearing is clear: by making Rembrandt the employee of his son and wife (who, in the eyes of the world, was still his servant) it protected him once and for all from pursuit by his creditors. In fact, Rembrandt had been able to reimburse only four of them. The others had seen nothing, firstly because the proceeds from the sale had been so insignificant, and secondly because Titus' new guardian had managed to get a fairly large portion of these proceeds set aside for his ward (who was not to receive the money until later). In any case, from now on nobody could lay claim to any part of Rembrandt's property.

118 *Titus reading.* About 1657

Thus, a situation which would normally have been humiliating for him was in fact a refuge. This he owed entirely to the exemplary honesty and solicitude of his wife and son.

A few days after this agreement had been signed, the house in the Breestraat was paid for by its new owner. This must have meant that the painter and his family could now delay their departure no longer. They moved out to a house in the Rozengracht and there Rembrandt continued his work; he also retained a few pupils, among them Aert de Gelder, but generally speaking young artists henceforth looked elsewhere for their instruction, to places where contemporary tastes were better satisfied.

CHAPTER NINETEEN

Fruits of solitude

As with his self-portraits, a link can be established between most of the compositions which Rembrandt produced in the years 1656—1660 and the events of his life during that period. *David harping before Saul, Christ at the Column, Jacob wrestling with the Angel, Moses breaking the Tables of the Law,* and *St Peter denying Christ* were all subjects which must naturally have suggested themselves to him at the time.

His purpose in painting *David harping before Saul* (c. 1657) was obviously to depict the mental torment and the relief, albeit accompanied by tears, which art is able to bring to the depressed and lonely man. Beyond doubt, the great powers of suggestion of this picture are due to Rembrandt's personal experience of these two feelings. Bowed down by melancholy, the King is seated holding a fold of the heavy curtain which hangs behind him. He conceals half his face as he wipes his left eye with it; the right eye blazes with anxiety. His long, thin, nervous hand rests limply on the shaft of a spear, incapable of throwing it at the target of his jealousy. Beside this man, impressive both in his size and in the splendour of his robes,

Ill. 116

David looks small, but the combination of light and shade on his own features gives him the rather demoniac appearance of a sorcerer. Rembrandt now knew that stirring, and even soothing, art could arise only from a mind from which serenity and peacefulness were excluded.

In the picture of about 1630 on the same subject (Städelsches Kunstinstitut, Frankfurt) Rembrandt had still adhered to the text of the Bible and made David into a rather pretty youth, while Saul was merely a man giving him a nasty look and holding the spear in his hand with menacing firmness. The psychological situation in the later work is thus far more complex and appreciably more moving.

Naturally, the second version is also richer in pictorial qualities. Saul's turban is painted in oranges and blue-greens of subtly different shades, and his clothes in golds and reds which are dark in some places and light in others. There is something warm and sumptuous about the harmonies, and they at once reveal that this is a scene with the atmosphere of tragic legends.

The *Christ at the Column* of 1658 was Rembrandt's third version of this theme, and also the most eloquent. The first (if the attribution of this work to Rembrandt is in fact correct) was executed about 1628. It features a Christ whose face expresses distress, but whose bare body is completely without poignancy. Clinical relief and anonymous draughtsmanship combine to make this a cold body, and on it falls a superficial chiaroscuro. In the second version (c. 1646) the body is emaciated; it gives an impression of chilliness which reveals Christ's apprehension while waiting with dread for the moment of torture. Yet it has a juvenile appearance which reminds one more of St Sebastian than of Christ.

The bare Christ in the 1658 work is also puny, but this time he is instantly recognizable as the man whom Pilate has handed over to the soldiers to be flogged. In the second version Christ was the only character; in the first there was a soldier standing guard over him; now there are two torturers at his side, one of whom is just completing the task of binding his feet together, while the other is getting ready to hoist him with a tug on the rope which is wound round his hands and over a pulley. This pulley forms the apex of a triangle in which the three characters are contained, but the fact that one of the torturers is standing and the other has one knee on the ground produces a most expressive asymmetrical effect. The kneeling man is so to speak invited to stand up and fill the gap above him, and it is clear that, as soon as he does so, he will attack the body of Christ in the centre of the canvas, where it describes a pale, trembling vertical soon about to quiver still more under the stretching of the rope. Thus Rembrandt does not depict the flagellation itself, he merely presages it. For an artist who, in *The Blinding of Samson,* portrayed brutality with such relish, this is significant. He now seems to shrink away from it; at any rate, he takes care not to show the act of brutality itself.

The distaste with which Rembrandt henceforth viewed violent acts is demonstrated equally clearly in *Jacob wrestling with the Angel* and *Moses breaking the Tables of the Law,* two paintings of around 1659 which cannot be counted among his finest works. In the first, there is so little movement and the expression on Jacob's face is so dispassionate that it is hard to believe there is a struggle in progress. Yet both these subjects were of a kind which must have been particularly dear to Rembrandt at the time. He too was wrestling with the angel and refusing to be overthrown. How close he must have felt to Moses as well! He must have been disposed to share the pained anger of a man who stands alone for truth against the errors of the crowd seduced by the worship of the golden calf. Nevertheless, for Rembrandt the time for expressions of violence was over: from now on his natural inclinations were for situations in which drama, while not necessarily any less intense, took a more restrained form.

Thus, in *St Peter denying Christ* (1660) the whole scene is evoked by the expression of the eyes, the light, and a few very sparing gestures. Nothing could be simpler and at the same time more eloquent than the servant bringing up her candle to St Peter's face to examine it, while he would prefer to be lost in the shadow. Other eyes are trained on the apostle—the two soldiers in the foreground are weighing him up with interest and suspicion and, in the background, Christ has turned round to witness his prophecy coming true. In the background the light is weak and wavering but in the centre of the canvas the light cast by the candle is fairly bright. It falls most strongly on the servant's bodice and St Peter's shoulder, but so close is the light to the saint's face that it threatens to force it from the semi-darkness. This threat can be felt just as strongly by the onlooker as by the apostle, whose features reflect confusion. The servant holds the candle in her left hand, with her right hand cupped round it: her index finger is almost translucent, its edges bright red from the flame behind. Placed as it is near St Peter's face, it seems to symbolize the burning anguish felt by the man whom fear has led to deny his master.

Yet if these five paintings were probably directly suggested to Rembrandt by the painful experiences of the years 1656—1660, he produced others which are seemingly independent of the events which troubled his life at the time. Among them is a work which depicts *Esther's Feast* (1660). Having invited Ahasuerus and Haman to dinner, Esther has just told the King that Haman intends to persecute her and her people. One can imagine the gestures and facial expressions which Rembrandt would formerly have felt obliged to use to convey the shocked surprise of a moment so full of pathos. Here he merely paints the silence which follows Esther's revelation. There is no more than a bare suggestion of anger in the look which Ahasuerus casts in Haman's direction, while Haman himself sits with head bowed, shattered by the unexpected accusation. Already a void cuts him off from the King, already he is partly consigned to darkness, whereas Esther is flooded with light and close to Ahasuerus. Bending slightly forward, she forms with him a triangular shape through which the artist makes the ties which unite the two characters immediately apparent.

In 1661 Rembrandt painted another banquet which again features a dramatic situation. This time he shows twelve Batavian conspirators grouped around their leader Julius Civilis taking an oath of rebellion against the Romans. Although swords are raised, the gestures and the facial expressions are restrained. Rembrandt was commissioned to paint this subject by the City Fathers of Amsterdam, who wished to decorate the gallery of the new Town Hall.

As it happened, he was not their first choice. They wanted to entrust the whole of the decoration to Govert Flinck, a former pupil of Rembrandt's who was known to be easier to deal with. But Flinck died in 1660, and it was then decided to share out the commission which was to have been his among a number of artists. The subjects for the pictures were suggested by the poet Vondel, who took them from Tacitus.

119 *The Conspiracy of Julius Civilis.* 1661

When Rembrandt completed his composition and presented it to
the municipality, the response was anything but enthusiastic; in fact,
they asked the artist to take the canvas back and modify it. Although
Rembrandt agreed to take it back, he not surprisingly refused to
make any changes. It remained untouched until, finding it too much
of an encumbrance, he cut it up and disposed of all but the piece
which has come down to us. The town-councillors of Amsterdam,
for their part, wasted no time in correcting the error they had made
in commissioning such an unobliging artist: a short while later the
position which had been reserved for Rembrandt's picture was filled
by a work by Juriaen Ovens, a painter who hardly warrants a
mention in present-day histories of Dutch art.

120 *An Angel dictating the Gospel to St Matthew.* 1661

121 *Self-portrait as St Paul.* 1661

All things considered, however, the town-councillors' disappointment was perfectly natural. Instead of presenting them with ancestors of whom they could feel proud, Rembrandt offered mere bumpkins. Each of these faces is primitive and coarse, and there is something savage as well as majestic about their leader—his blind eye even makes him look cruel and intimidating. The roughness of the characters is accentuated by the manner in which they are painted. Some of them are mere outlines, and throughout the relief is effected by broad strokes. Yet the very characteristics which can only have displeased lovers of an over-polished treatment and an idealized reconstruction of history make this painting, for modern eyes, one of the most impressive works Rembrandt ever produced. There was really only one way of bringing such an episode to life, and that was to present it in a visionary style; otherwise these men would have appeared to be merely actors on a stage rather than real heroes who look genuinely capable of taking dangerous, passionate action.

Here again, the main factor which gives the picture its power of expression is the light. At first sight its source appears to be behind the character with the goblet in his outstretched hand who sits against the light with his back to the onlooker. Then one notices that it is not merely artificial but unreal. It seems to emanate from the tablecloth itself, which has an incandescent appearance. Once more the play of the light has a freedom which goes beyond all the requirements of realism. It not only strikes the bodies, it penetrates them and transforms their substance. This has the simultaneous effect of giving the characters a look of fantasy which places them firmly in the past, and also a fascinating presence which bestows on this episode from ancient history the impact of a modern event.

Ill. 119 It must not, however, be forgotten that only a fragment of the original composition remains. Originally, as a drawing reveals, the table was positioned on a dais in the middle of a great vaulted room taking up two-thirds of the height of the picture. This made the characters look further away and quite small in relation to the work as a whole, whereas in the fragment which has survived they occupy almost the entire surface of the canvas. Moreover, the work was intended to be hung at a particular height, and Rembrandt tried to take into account the fact that it would be seen from a distance. He thus had various reasons for painting *The Conspiracy of Julius Civilis* in a bold style, and it is quite natural that in his ordinary studio paintings the treatment should be of a different character.

In fact, most of the works of this period were not paintings of a scene but portraits or faces which stemmed from Rembrandt's imagination (usually based on a model). Thus, since painting *Christ at Emmaus* in 1648, he had produced some ten half-length portraits of young Jews who, under his brush, had been transformed into as many Christs. Half of them probably date from the period 1656–1661. Generally they have dark hair, a dark beard, and a sad, careworn expression, but in the last of the series the hair is fair, and the face brighter, more assured, and less touching.

For whom did he paint these works? For whom, furthermore, did he portray a woman in a nun's habit and two hooded monks looking like Franciscans, one of whom has the features of Titus? Did he decide to paint them on his own account, or was he commissioned to do them by a Catholic, of whom there were still some left in the Netherlands? Whatever the answer, these works provide further proof that Rembrandt did not concern himself with being an orthodox Protestant.

During this period he also executed a series of Apostles, some of them works of outstanding interest. The main quality of his *St Bartholomew* and *St Matthew*, both of 1661, is their spiritual fervour, *Ill. 120* but *St John*, which is also known as *The Evangelist writing*, is one of the most remarkable canvases of this period. Rejecting the rather facile effects which portraits of grey-bearded old men produce, Rembrandt depicts a young man whose oval face has nothing picturesque about it—so much so that a later generation thought it necessary to make it look older by adding a beard. But what spiritual concentration there is in the features, how monumental are the shapes and how eloquent the simplicity!

Among these Apostles is a *St Paul* (1661)—clearly a self-portrait— *Ill. 121* which is totally different from the usual portrayal of this character. Rembrandt himself had produced a painting of St Paul a few years previously in which his normal appearance was preserved. In the 1661 work, however, all his fire and enterprise have disappeared. This man seems to be thinking of anything but spreading a doctrine, gathering followers to the faith and organizing a church; rather than wishing to bring his influence to bear upon the world, he looks more

122 *Two Negroes.* 1661

inclined to flee it. There is something fearful in his expression. He looks not only humble but humiliated and, if he knows the truth, it is not exhilarating, but painful and depressive. It consists in the conviction that life is harsh, and that one needs an almost inhuman stubbornness not to be completely overcome by its buffetings. One must, however, be wary of basing an opinion of Rembrandt's state of mind in 1661 on this one work. There may have been moments when weariness came over him, but he was still capable of regaining possession of himself. After all, this picture was not to be his last.

Ill. 122   Although Rembrandt's *Two Negroes* (or two studies of the same Negro) bears the date 1661, the style of the work suggests that it may actually have been executed earlier. However that may be, the painting is a compelling one in every way. For its originality to be fully appreciated, it has to be compared to a similar picture which Rubens (or van Dyck) had produced about fourteen years before. The Flemish artist had been chiefly interested in the structure of the head, which he had considered from four different angles, and, all in all, the painting is a document for ethnologists (albeit a fine one) rather than a revelation of the essential Negro character. Rembrandt, on the contrary, revealed the very soul of the black race, at least as it was in certain circumstances outside Africa, particularly in the 17th century when slave-traders sold tens thousands of Negroes into servitude in the American colonies. It is true that those whom a happy twist of fortune brought to Holland were released, as slavery there was forbidden, but apart from the fact that such Negroes were not numerous, they must have found it difficult to forget the fate from which they had escaped.

The half-open mouth which seems to be panting, the startled and resigned look in the eyes, that mysterious noble quality which invariably characterizes the victim, these are the features by which Rembrandt contrives to render the essence of these men who have been transplanted to a world which is not their own. To have been able to paint such a magnificent work, Rembrandt must obviously have regarded these Negroes with sympathy, a sympathy made all the more profound by the fact that he detected in them a feeling which he himself knew well—that of living in an environment to which one is ill-adapted.

This indeed is a feeling which he tended to share more and more with his models, even with those hardly likely to have experienced it. In this respect nothing could be more significant than his *Portrait of Jacob Trip*. Trip was a merchant from Dordrecht who was probably neither more nor less rich in inner life than other merchants he had portrayed in the 1630s. There are strong grounds for saying this, as the same model was portrayed by another artist, Nicolaes Maes, at around the same time. Maes painted Trip as the ordinary observer would have seen him, and the result is someone who certainly knows how to conduct his business affairs and gain the respect of his fellow-men, but who does not compel recognition as a deep thinker. In short, Maes in 1660 produced the kind of portrait which Rembrandt would have painted about 1635, but which he had now abandoned. In this work, Jacob Trip has ceased to be a merchant of

Dordrecht and becomes instead a patriarch, a contemporary of the Old Testament Jacob.

Thus, whereas there had formerly been a clear difference between the portraits which featured the artist's compatriots and those which depicted Jews, sometimes presented as biblical characters, this distinction now ceased to exist. Henceforth, to a greater or lesser degree, Rembrandt removed all his models from their natural element, stripping them of the mediocrity of their position in life and introducing them to a world where they could lead a more reflective existence and where their spiritual qualities were more highly developed.

Indeed, there is no longer any real difference between the merchant Jacob Trip and the *Rabbi* of 1657–1660, a figure illuminated by mature spirituality. The picture displays the rather bitter wisdom born of repeated comparison of things as they are and things as they ought to be, of what strong moral principles require and what the frailties of human nature allow.

Even more than in the portraits of Jews which he executed around 1650, clothing has here lost its previous importance. All the picturesqueness of fabrics which he once took such pleasure in bringing out he now sacrifices to immaterial things, to sparkles of light and secretive shadows.

During the 1630s, as we have seen, Rembrandt revealed secrets in his drawings of which he gave not the slightest indication in his paintings. In fact, his drawings at this stage of his life became less frequent and also revealed less than before about his private troubles, no doubt because they had come to be displayed so fully in his paintings. Yet his drawings and etchings still deserve to be considered with the greatest interest, for they continue to show sides of Rembrandt's activity which would not otherwise be known.

His *Woman seated at a Window* (c. 1657) is one drawing which does seem to have been inspired by the hard times through which he and his family were living. The woman—possibly Hendrickje herself—is pensive; painful thoughts bow down her head and dull her gaze. Retired within herself, skull and body shrouded in white and standing out against a dark background, she seems to be oblivious of all but her own misfortunes. She makes no effort to look attractive. The very style of the work is characterized by its roughness. So thick, stiff and summary are the lines that they give the impression of being drawn with the wood of the brush, not with the hairs. Yet their very harshness and inexorability are an admirable match for the misfortune which weighs down her bowed head.

Although *Girl sleeping* is related to *Woman seated at a Window,* it lacks the latter's roughness. The line is bold, but not without flexibility. Drawn this time with the brush, it possesses a liveliness, economy and diversity such as one associates with the wash-drawings of old Chinese artists. Thick and hasty in places, light and careful in others, it manages to evoke not only a woman in a sleeping position, but her sleep itself.

There is no sign of Rembrandt's troubles either in this work or in the *Nude Studies* which he drew between 1658 and 1661. These bodies have the firm, attractive flesh of youth. Of course, the artist no more sets out to idealize them here than in his early works, but he is not so insistent on emphasizing the features which are not ideal. The attitude of his *Naked Woman sitting on a. Stool,* for instance, is similar to that of the *Naked Woman sitting on a Mound* of around 1630, but he now takes care to place her right forearm in such a position that the belly is hidden, whereas in the earlier work he brought out its heaviness and its folds of flesh so strongly. The draughtsmanship in another study, a *Woman seated on a Bed* with her right arm raised above her head, is even more delicate and flexible. Here Rembrandt does not attempt to encircle the body with a line which gives it a rather stiff shape and cuts it off from its surroundings. Similarly, the light which strikes her naked body is not at all harsh and helps to make it attractive.

Ill. 123
Ill. 23

Ill. 124

But these are all drawings, where execution is generally less elaborate than in etchings. In his etched treatments of nudes, shape is rather more sharply defined, yet Rembrandt refrains from showing many anatomical details. One of these women is bare only to the waist; she is sitting by a stove, with her head leaning slightly forward and an expression of vague anxiety on her face. It has been inferred from this that she is in a doctor's consulting room. However valid this interpretation may be, these nudes have certain characteristics in common: they are true to life; they do not pose; they have no desire to impress the onlooker; they have the supreme naturalness of those who know they are alone, and who exist only for themselves, without affectation or self-satisfaction.

123 *Naked Woman sitting on a Stool.* 1658

124 *Woman seated on a Bed.* 1658

125 *Negress lying down.* 1658

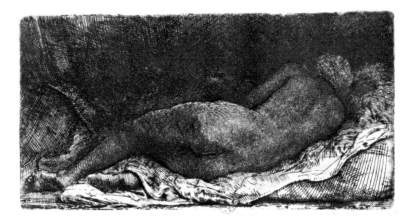

126 *The Woman with the Arrow.* 1661

When Rembrandt came to etch a recumbent nude, he no longer thought of portraying the evident eagerness of a Danaë to give herself up to passion. Instead he depicted a sleeping Antiope unaware of the approach of Jupiter. Alternatively, avoiding all reference to mythology, he showed the reclining body of a negress from the back, her supple, dark flesh more in shadow than illuminated.

Ill. 125

Another nude seen from the back, but this time seated, is *The Woman with the Arrow* (1661). This was the last but one of his etchings, the final one, a portrait, not being produced until 1665. A winding outline marks off the outer edges of the body which is bathed in light, but a light which has nothing garish about it, and is not used to heighten a cruel realism. In fact, it replaces all the body's possible imperfections, while the shadows mould its shapes gently, making it even more attractive. Because of the arrow, which has been taken for that of Cupid, it has been suggested that this nude is Venus. But while the possibility that Rembrandt had Venus in mind certainly cannot be ruled out, as usual he made no attempt to deify the body; he merely regarded it with tenderness.

Ill. 126

A new ordeal

On 7 August 1661, Hendrickje again went to see a notary, this time because she was ill and wished to make a will. She decided to make her daughter Cornelia her residuary legatee; if she, in turn, were to die without a natural heir, everything was to revert to her half-brother Titus. Rembrandt was nominated as Cornelia's guardian, and was authorized to take whatever he thought fit on her behalf, without being answerable to any other person. Hendrickje expressed the wish that the business established on 15 December 1660 should be carried on by Titus and his father for as long as Rembrandt desired. She expressed the further wish that, in the event of the inheritance falling to Titus, Rembrandt should enjoy its usufruct for the duration of his life—but she also specified that this usufruct was only intended for his food and keep, and could not be seized by his creditors. In effect, then, Hendrickje placed her entire wealth at Rembrandt's disposal, ignoring his inability to manage his affairs and the fact that she was exposing her daughter to the risk of seeing the inheritance elude her.

Hendrickje did not die for some time after her last will and testament were recorded. On 20 October 1661 she was cited as a

127 *The Syndics of the Clothmakers' Guild.* 1662

witness in a document whose only interest lies in the information that she was still in fact alive at that date (she is here referred to, incidentally, as Rembrandt's wife, which seems to indicate that it had at last been decided to recognize her real, even if not legal, position). Hendrickje's death should probably be situated in 1662, for on 27 October of that year Rembrandt sold Saskia's tomb in the Oude Kerk, presumably in order to be able to buy another one for Hendrickje in the Westerkerk (Western Church)—there was a regulation in force in Amsterdam at the time according to which the dead had to be buried in the nearest church. If Rembrandt really could not afford the dues which he would have had to pay to have Hendrickje buried beside Saskia, if he felt he really must sell one tomb to have enough money to buy another, his financial position, once more, must have been less than mediocre.

128 *Homer.* 1663

Indeed, documents of the time again speak of loans, arrangements, disputes, trials—and works by Rembrandt which were sold for absurdly low prices. In August 1662, 36 guilders were paid for one of his paintings in Amsterdam, while a few months previously, in the Hague, 73 of his etchings had fetched three guilders and one sou. It is true that a poem of the same year written in glory of Amsterdam mentioned him as first among the city's painters, but, as the prices just quoted make quite clear, this was an opinion which was by no means universally held.

Was it shared by the syndics of the Clothmakers' Guild? At any Ill. 127 rate, they commissioned Rembrandt to paint their portrait—probably making it plain that they did not wish to be treated in the same way as Captain Frans Banning Cocq's harquebusiers. There is nothing fanciful about the arrangement—five characters grouped behind a table and a sixth in the background. All are dressed in black costumes with large white collars and all, apart from the figure in the background, wear broad hats which are also black. Similarly, all are portrayed facing full-on or at a three-quarters angle, and all look towards the front, as though we had burst into the room where they are in session, and they were demanding an explanation for our sudden appearance. The result is not only a psychological tension which creates a link between the characters, but also a direct dialogue between each of them and ourselves. Nevertheless, these are not features which express a merely transitory feeling; they reveal that there are interesting and individual minds beneath. Everything points to the conclusion that the syndics owed these very arresting spiritual qualities entirely to Rembrandt, but the fact that he felt able to impart them is the important thing. Formerly an insignificant model would have warranted a dull portrait obviously executed on a commission basis.

In any event, this picture of 1662 is far superior in quality to the normal Dutch group portrait. Only Frans Hals' *Regents* and *Regentesses of the Old Men's Home* are in the same class. Indeed, the comparison with Frans Hals is an illuminating one in every way, for it underlines the originality which both he and Rembrandt attained towards the end of their careers. Whereas Hals is harsh, vengeful and pitiless to his models, Rembrandt regards them with sympathy. And while the Haarlem painter uses a colouring whose restraint

129 *Self-portrait.* 1665

verges on the austere (mainly blacks, greys and a dark purple), Rembrandt sets off the browns of the background, the whites and greys, and the blacks of the costumes by a wide red and ochre carpet whose radiance gives warmth to the whole work.

Certain of Rembrandt's drawings bear a relation to *The Syndics of the Clothmakers' Guild,* drawings which show isolated characters in attitudes different from those in the picture. Although the grouping of the six men may look simple, therefore, it did not come about by accident. The structure comprises triangles, verticals and above all horizontals, which bring calm and stability to the composition. The drawings are of interest for yet another reason, as they illustrate Rembrandt's style towards the end of his career as a draughtsman— in the last years of his life nearly all his works were paintings. The reason for this was probably that his eyesight was failing, and doubtless the same factor explains why, in his last drawings, his strokes are no longer supple and fluent. Rembrandt was now drawing them with a reed-pen, and the instrument he used obviously determined their character. Thus, whereas in *The Circumcision* (c. 1663) the pen inscribes flexible and incisive lines on the paper, and in his *Study for One of the Syndics of the Clothmakers' Guild* (c. 1662) the brush produces a pictorial effect by working mainly in shaded patches of ink, in the *Portrait of a Man* (c. 1662) and *Noah's Ark* (c. 1660/62) the reed-pen creates a drawing characterized by stiffness and a rugged, rudimentary appearance, but also by subtly different outlines and an imposing vigour.

Homer reciting Verses (1661/62) is drawn with the brush, and is a work of extraordinary authority. There are many extremely varied lines—slow and quick, delicate and very firm—but they are not the chief means of expression. More important is the arrangement of light and dark, and all the gradations of wash. It is these features which make Homer into the massive, monumental shape he is, a majestic pyramidal form so strongly evocative of the narrator who celebrated the exploits of gods and heroes with such genius.

Ill. 128 This work was a study for a painting of 1663 which was so badly damaged in a fire that only the figure of *Homer* himself has survived. Here he looks much more strongly marked by the passage of time than in the drawing—Rembrandt stresses the withered flesh and the faded skin. He also brings out much better how Homer, deprived of visual contact with the outside world, can concentrate undisturbed on the epics he sees in his mind's eye, and which he relates through a wide, rather frightened mouth. His right shoulder is covered by a yellowish shawl which is the most vividly lit part of the whole work—in accordance with that method so dear to Rembrandt by which the point of brightest light is situated not in the face but beside it, in order to make it look more mysterious. At first sight, the light appears to strike the shawl, but the more one looks, the more one notices that it is the shawl itself which gives off this light, painted with an oily texture as luminous as pale gold.

Nine years before, *Aristotle contemplating the Bust of Homer* had so fired the Sicilian collector Antonio Ruffo with enthusiasm that he had decided he would like companion pictures to go with it, and in 1660/61 requested two highly regarded Italian artists, Guercino and Mattia Preti, to paint, respectively, a *Cosmographer* and a *Denis of Syracuse*. But he found this *Homer*, which he had commissioned, a disappointment; he thought it unfinished and accepted it only after first returning it to the artist. After this experience he never again gave Rembrandt a commission. Furthermore, although he was still to buy a considerable number of Rembrandt's prints, he bought no more of his paintings. Ruffo was not the only person to feel that Rembrandt left his paintings unfinished; at a time when classical tendencies were the fashion—as they had been in the Netherlands since the 1650s—many people subscribed to this opinion. Rembrandt did not allow himself to be put off by these criticisms. He had never worried much about the objections of his clients, and now he worried even less. What, in the opinion of some, were faults, were in fact the very qualities which enabled him to produce his most profound and pungent works.

Thus, of all the characters who have been identified as Apostles, the *Evangelist writing* of the Boymans-van Beuningen Museum, Rotterdam, is one of the freest in treatment, and also one of the most admirable. Older than *St John writing,* less serene, and less sure of his inspiration, the evangelist casts an inscrutable look in the spectator's direction. The light shows up only half his face, and instead of making the features clear it blurs them slightly, preventing us from fully understanding this fascinating but uncommunicative figure. The paint is no less rich than in *Homer,* and at the same time

130 *The Jewish Bride*. About 1665

more refined. Among the tints, it is not ochres or browns but reds which predominate. They appear in the cap and the garment, their restrained warmth made only slightly brighter by light oranges.

What of Rembrandt himself at this stage? The *Self-Portrait* of 1664 reveals an old man's face of many wrinkles and tanned, hardened skin. Yet he looks more peaceful in mind and less bitter than he had around 1660—he gives the impression of having come to terms with fate. Is this weariness, or an indifference brought about by excessive suffering? At any rate, he is still standing; he will clearly continue to resist, as he will continue to paint. In another *Self-Portrait* executed a short while later, he even manages a laugh. True, this is by no means a laugh of gaiety, rather of derision. It is the crumpled face of an old clown, and he puts on a grin which is forced and, all in all, pathetic. Was he laughing at a society whose preoccupations seemed to him to be ridiculous, or at life, which had buffeted him so much without ever succeeding in overthrowing him? Or simply at himself, a man of less than 60 years of age who looked 70, but who was still there, bruised and battered but as tenacious as a cat?

In any event, he had never painted himself with more dash and never cared so little for what is normally known as beauty. The face

Ill. 129

245

looks as though it has been moulded in clay by quick, vigorous hands. The paint is generous, but the range of colours small—mainly ochres on a dark background. Yet the ochres are so varied in shade and the rough edges of the paint, sometimes sparingly, sometimes thickly applied, catch the light at such a variety of angles that the work possesses a dull, savage intensity.

CHAPTER TWENTY-ONE

Last years

Early in 1665 Titus had the satisfaction of winning a lawsuit that had been in progress for several years: a former creditor of his father's, Isaac van Hertsbeeck, who had been paid back 4200 guilders at the time of Rembrandt's bankruptcy, was now obliged to return the money, it being decided by the court that it was Titus' by right. Titus' final share in the bankruptcy amounted to almost 7000 guilders, which were remitted to him in November of the same year. From now on Rembrandt and his family were thus relieved of material worries. Rembrandt could even contemplate buying more works of art, which he never seems to have lost the desire to possess—a letter of 15 October 1666 informs us that he had offered 1000 guilders for a Holbein.

This change in his material circumstances probably also explains his neglect of a commission which he no doubt accepted at a time when he could ill afford to refuse it. Indeed, the subject of this work—*Juno*—is one which is hardly likely to have corresponded to his own tastes. To paint a *Flora* in which he saw a pretext to adorn

131 *Lucretia.* 1666

Saskia or Hendrickje with flowers, or even to paint *Venus and Cupid* when it gave him the opportunity to portray two people whom he held dear was something Rembrandt could do with enthusiasm, but the haughty, jealous, vindictive Juno was a different matter. In 1665 the man who had commissioned the canvas complained that it had not yet been completed. Nor was it delivered in the following year, or in fact at any time before Rembrandt's death, when it figured in the inventory of objects found in his house. It may be that he kept it because he was not fully satisfied. This would certainly be understandable, for this Juno is plainly nothing more than a sensual, arrogant, narrow-minded bourgeoise.

In his painting of *Lucretia,* on the other hand, it is immediately *Ill. 131* apparent that Rembrandt was moved by the fate of this young woman who was raped and then committed suicide. He depicted this subject on two separate occasions, first in 1664 and again in 1666. In the earlier work Lucretia's face is reminiscent of Hendrickje's. But her attitude tries a little too hard to be eloquent. Both arms raised to breast height, one hand holding the dagger and the other open, her posture looks more like that of a tragedienne on a stage than a desperate woman who kills herself in her loneliness. In contrast, no undue emphasis mars the second version. Lucretia clasps a curtain cord in her left hand, as though she were afraid of collapsing after having plunged the dagger into her heart. Pain and determination are written in her features. The inflexibility of her decision is also evoked by the vertical position of the head and the folds of the chemise, which fills the centre of the canvas with a broad patch of light.

It was probably shortly before this second *Lucretia* that Rembrandt executed one of the finest works of his career. It has been given the name *The Jewish Bride,* although in fact it has not been *Ill. 130* possible to identify the two characters portrayed. A variety of interpretations have been put forward—Isaac and Rebecca, Jacob and Rachel, Boaz and Ruth, Tobias and Sarah, Titus and his bride-to-be Magdalena van Loo, the Jewish poet Miguel de Barrios and his wife Abigael de Pina have all been suggested. The models remain unknown, the characters enigmatic. But more important than their identity, in any case, are the sentiments which Rembrandt expresses through them.

132 *Woman holding a Carnation*. About 1668

133 *Lady holding an Ostrich-feather Fan.* About 1667

The man is leaning slightly towards the woman, whose features express shyness and reserve. He rests one hand on her shoulder and the other on her breast, a gesture of great delicacy very different from the one Rembrandt himself had once made in the portrait with Saskia on his lap. He was an owner asserting his authority; this man is a protector and a confidant. In *The Jewish Bride*, moreover, there is not a trace of sensuality, merely affection and an unutterable tenderness. The eyes of the models do not meet: they are too absorbed by inward feelings to wish to look at each other. They have no need of visual contact, for emotionally they are united.

Such a psychological reality, of course, is hardly a characteristic of a young engaged couple. It is the product of a man of long experience and great suffering who has had the opportunity to see things for what they are really worth, and who has reached the conclusion that nothing is more precious than warm affection.

So rich and intense is the inner life in this picture that even the many jewels with which the young woman is adorned assume a special significance. Despite the beauty of the pearls, and the rings and gold bracelets studded with precious stones, one looks upon them less as worldly finery than as the accessories to a rite, for everything in this painting is endowed with spiritual meaning. Even more than by the facial expressions, this impression is conveyed by the colouring. Two colours predominate—red, of which gentle streaks appear in the woman's face and a brilliant splash in her dress, and gold, which, particularly on the man's arm, gives off a very delicate, soft light. In parts the paint is so thick that the canvas is dotted with many rough edges, but far from making it dull or tarnished they only serve to heighten its brilliance.

Although he relished the freedom which he could display with characters created by his own imagination, Rembrandt nevertheless continued to paint straight portraits. In 1665 he portrayed the painter Gerard de Lairesse. Lairesse was a young man of 25 from Liege who had just arrived in Amsterdam and who later, in the name of French classicism, was to condemn the master whom at first he had admired—any chance of immortality he may have, however, he owes more to this portrait than to his own pictures. Another painter who was to write about Rembrandt, Samuel van Hoogstraten, is believed to be the model of a work executed in 1666. In the same year Rembrandt produced a portrait of the poet Jeremias de Decker, a friend of his who had devoted some verse to his art and who was to write a further poem hailing him as 'The Apelles of his time'.

Although this latter portrait is a fine work, Rembrandt's genius is even more imposingly displayed in his *Portrait of a Gentleman with Gloves* (c. 1667) and *Man with a Magnifying-Glass* (c. 1668) and in their companion pictures *Lady holding an Ostrich-feather Fan* and *Woman holding a Carnation*. It used to be thought that *Man with a Magnifying-Glass* was a portrait of Titus or Spinoza. In fact, at the time when the picture was painted in 1668, both of them were younger than the character depicted—Titus was 27 and Spinoza 36. Moreover, Spinoza had had to leave Amsterdam in 1656 and there is no evidence that Rembrandt ever came into contact with him. Yet, it is true that this head gnawed by anxiety and ennobled by spiritual passion could very well be that of a philosopher. But the face of the *Gentleman with Gloves* also shines with a rich inner life, as do the characters in earlier works also—from which the only conclusion which can be drawn is that this was far more a product of the artist himself than a quality innate in his models.

Ill. 133
Ill. 132

Although the *Lady holding an Ostrich-feather Fan* does not yet appear to have lived long enough to experience in any intensity the pathetic side of the human situation, she seems to have a presentiment of that pathos and to be dreading it. Her eyes stare at an unknown target, her mouth is limp and fearful. This is not the only distinguishing feature of the picture. Compared with the *Portrait of a Fashionable Young Lady* of 1639, which is somewhat recalls, it is noticeable that the clothing is less elegant and the style more free.

The *Woman holding a Carnation* is even more moving. Her face reveals a mind less haughty and less feverish than that of the *Man with a Magnifying-Glass,* and her expression is a little sad but comforting. The blazing red carnation in her right hand may be intended to symbolize a beauty unaffected by human anxieties whose existence Rembrandt advises us not to forget. At any rate, the woman presents it delicately, and it is the most vivid point in the picture. But other more subdued shades of red in the dress give the painting its subtle warmth.

Is the model in this portrait the same woman who figures in the *Family Group* of the Brunswick Museum, which also dates from

Ill. 134

134 *Family Group*. About 1668

around 1668? The shape of the two faces is fairly similar, but the mother in the *Family Group* looks younger. According to the art historian W. R. Valentiner she should be identified as Magdalena van Loo, the wife of Titus, and the little girl on her lap as her daughter Titia. Again, according to Valentiner's thesis, the other characters in the portrait are Cornelia (Hendrickje's daughter) and Titia's tutor François van Bijlert and his son. However, this theory collapses as soon as one refers to the dates. Titus married Magdalena on 10 February 1668, Titia was christened on 22 March 1669, and 7 months later Rembrandt was dead—but the little girl in this picture is unquestionably more than seven months old.

In any case, considerations of this kind do not merit such close attention. The important thing is not the names of the models but the feelings to which the painting gives outward form. The affectionate and rather worried look of the mother and the way in which she touches the child reveal Rembrandt's belief that a child is a fragile creature whom parents are always in danger of losing. Again, therefore, the painting expresses not an objective reality but his own subjective experience. A second characteristic of his most significant models reappears in this work—they do not wholly belong to the age in which they live. When Rubens portrayed Hélène Fourment with two of her children, he showed her as contemporaries must have known her—an elegant young woman who was clearly pleased to be the wife of a great painter. But the family in Rembrandt's work appear in that atmosphere of legend which has already been so frequently encountered. He seems almost to have painted not a mother but *the* mother, with all the grave, semi-religious overtones with which the word is endowed in ancient literature and no doubt it was again his Bible-reading which suggested such an image to him. But his development as a painter was also responsible for its creation—the picture's strong legendary tone is in part due to the almost complete lack of realism in its style.

Of course, it is still possible to distinguish faces, hands and clothes, but the style is bolder and more allusive than ever before. The mother's dress is the best example of this; one is more conscious of the feel of the paint than of that of the fabrics, and the trails of colour are more obvious than the folds of the garment. The bright colours are even richer and more varied than in *The Jewish Bride*— *Ill. 130* a mixture of brick red, salmon pink, olive green and greenish blue. But the predominant tints are warm, like the feelings.

It was also towards the end of his life that Rembrandt treated, for the first time in a painting, a subject which had appeared in a print as early as 1636 and shortly afterwards in drawings—*The Return of the Prodigal Son*. In the etching, the bitterness felt by the father at his son's departure does not seem to have been entirely dissipated by the joy of his homecoming, but in the picture the old man's expression reveals only emotion, gentleness and affection. Facing the front, he bends down over his son, who has his back turned to us, an arrangement which binds the two men more closely together than in the etching and the drawings, where they are shown in profile.

Four characters are present at the scene. Two of them are standing back in the shadow, the main function of their faces being to introduce a little light there. The other two can be seen better, but hardly have they been noticed before one is led to follow their example and concentrate on the main characters. In the etching Rembrandt had still been anxious to emphasize that the father runs to meet his son; he had depicted the servant bringing the son some clothes; he had brought out the surprise and curiosity which his return arouses. In the painting the onlookers are merely silent and still. In other words, true to the general tendency of his later work, he relied less on narrative and more on suggestion, he was less concerned to describe an action than to express states of mind. And the role of the two ancillary characters who have such a biblical look about them (although the Bible does not include them in this parable) is precisely to give greater emphasis to the feelings which Rembrandt wishes to illustrate.

Another old man no less affected by emotion than the father of the prodigal son, but more frail, figures in what was almost certainly Rembrandt's last painting. He was a character who had followed Rembrandt throughout his career: *Simeon in the Temple*. He had first appeared in a painting of around 1628, then in another painting of 1631, and finally in an etching of about 1654. Never before, however, had he been accorded a position of such prominence as in this picture. The only other person in the work is the Virgin; there is no High Priest to divert attention from him, no secondary character, not the least evocation of an architectural framework. He is practically alone with the Child he holds in his arms, illuminated by the consolation of his troubles. Thus, as in *The Prodigal Son*, the representation of an action has given way to the outward expression of a feeling. But *Simeon in the Temple* was never finished: how the definitive work would have appeared can thus only be surmised, but the treatment would surely have been less woolly, and the shapes less soft.

Indeed, Rembrandt's last *Self-Portrait*, which bears the date 1669, is far from lacking in firmness. Surprisingly, the features are well-rounded, and the face has a calm not to be found in any of the self-portraits of preceding years. Rembrandt now seems to have reached the stage of being impervious to suffering—or probably more cor-

Ill. 12
Ills 13, 108

rectly, he had passed that stage. Having been racked by it so often, he had found a refuge where it could no longer reach him, or at least where it no longer tormented him, where he accepted it as one of the calamities inherent in human existence.

Yet death had once more burst into his life, this time depriving him of someone he probably held more dear than any other person in the world—Titus. He was buried on 7 September 1668. Seven months previously Titus had been married, and when he died his wife was expecting a child, who was to be the Titia already mentioned. But Rembrandt was not to watch his granddaughter growing up for long. On 4 October 1669 he also died. Had he lived another fortnight, he would have found himself in a position similar to that which prevailed after Saskia's death—he would have been left to look after a baby less than one year old. For Magdalena, Titus' wife, did not survive for long either; she was buried on 21 October. Thus, only two children remained to represent Rembrandt's immediate family circle—Cornelia, the daughter of Hendrickje, and Titia, the daughter of Titus.

CHAPTER TWENTY-TWO

Survival

When, on 8 October 1669, Rembrandt's body was interred at the Westerkerk, how many people realized that Holland had just lost the greatest painter in her history? One can be almost certain that their number was very small. Rembrandt had moved too far apart from his fellow-men, he had ended up painting in a style which was too divergent from the tastes of most of his compatriots for it to be otherwise. Mention has already been made of two books published after his death and the opinions there expressed about *The Night Watch*. Other works appeared at the same time or a little later which are also revealing.

In 1675 the cosmopolitan painter of German origin Joachim von Sandrart had the first volume of his *Academia Tedesca dell'Architectura, Scultura et Pictura* published in Nuremberg. In connexion with Rembrandt, he relates what he saw and heard in Amsterdam between 1637 and 1645. 'One almost has to admire the fact', he writes, 'that despite being born in the country as the son of a miller, Rembrandt was so gifted for the fine arts that, through his great application, he reached a high level of achievement. His only trouble was that he never visited Italy and other places where antiques and the theory of art may be studied.' Thus 'he unhesitatingly set himself up against the rules of our art such as anatomy and the proportions of the human body, against perspective and the usefulness of antique statues, against the draughtsmanship of Raphael and against the academies so very necessary to our profession, maintaining that one should let oneself be guided only by nature and ignore all other rules'. Sandrart also mentions the income which Rembrandt received from his pupils and his own work, and goes on: 'It is certain that, had he been able to get on with people and behave in a reasonable manner, he would have been even wealthier. But although he was no spendthrift he could not uphold his social position: he always sought the company of people of a low order, something which also hindered him in his work.'

He deserves praise, Sandrart continues, for his fine use of colours. In this field, 'he has opened the eyes of those who are more dyers than painters, with their harsh, aggressive juxtaposition of garish colours.' After this word of praise Sandrart adds further reservations: 'Rembrandt depicted few ancient poems and few allegories or subjects taken from history; for the most part he painted over-simple things which do not provide much food for thought.'

Baldinucci, the author of the *Cominciamento* already quoted, also remarks that Rembrandt's colouring was of great distinction, but that his draughtsmanship was inferior to Govert Flinck's.

The Frenchman Roger de Piles expressed a similar opinion. In his *Cours de peinture par principes* (1718) he awarded Rembrandt 17 marks out of 20 for colour, but only 6 for draughtsmanship. In his *Abrégé de la vie des peintres, avec des réflexions sur leurs ouvrages* (1699), the same author, echoing Sandrart, said: 'One will not find in Rembrandt's work either the taste of Raphael or that of the ancients, or poetic thoughts or elegant draughtsmanship; one will merely find all that the Dutch national character, conceived by a vivid imagination, is capable of producing. Sometimes he raised it from its baseness by a flash of inspiration, but as he had no experience of fine proportion he easily relapsed into the bad taste to which he was accustomed.' To this criticism de Piles adds: 'He had a supreme understanding of chiaroscuro, while his local colours give each other mutual assistance and the comparison shows each of them off. In the subjects which he depicted his flesh-tints are no less realistic, fresh or studied than Titian's.'

Already before this Andries Pels, a compatriot of Rembrandt's, had written a poem in which he stressed the bad taste of the artist, whom he dubbed 'The first heretic in painting'. 'Rather than choose a Greek Venus as his model', said Pels, 'he chose instead a washer-woman or a peat-worker ... Flabby breasts, misshapen hands, even the marks of a corset round the back and of garters round the legs, all this he felt obliged to reproduce in order to be true to life.' In conclusion Pels observed: 'What a pity for art that such a talented man did not make better use of his gifts! Who would have surpassed him?'

Who would have surpassed him? Gerard de Lairesse, in his *Het Groot Schilderboek* (1707), mentioned people who had considered, and still considered, that Rembrandt had been the greatest painter of his time, that he had been able to accomplish everything which art and the brush allows, and that no one had yet managed to surpass him. Lairesse, however, was anxious to make it plain that he was quite definitely not of the same opinion. He did not deny that there had been a time when he thought very highly of Rembrandt's style, but at that period, he said, he had hardly begun to understand the infallible rules of art which, as everybody knew, were those of French classicism upheld by the Academy. He was thus forced to acknowledge his own errors and simultaneously repudiate those of Rembrandt—chiaroscuro, grey, yellow or russet shadows, impasto, in short, everything that constitutes his elder's originality.

Eleven years later there appeared the first volume of *Groote Schouburgh der Nederlantsche Konstschilders en Schilderessen*, a book written by Arnold Houbraken, a former pupil of Samuel van Hoogstraten. The author devotes a good deal of space to Rembrandt, and praises his ability to make his portraits look so life-like, and the inexhaustible power of invention which he exhibited for faces, attitudes and dress. But he also expresses certain regrets: Rembrandt left many paintings, and even more etchings, unfinished; he rarely painted hands in an appropriate manner; he ignored the fact that the naked body of a woman is the most marvellous subject which a brush can depict; finally, he did not accept the rules which it is important to adhere to, and his was not therefore an example to be followed.

Houbraken's opinion that on many occasions Rembrandt failed to complete his paintings was clearly due to the fact that he was unable to detect in them the finish of an overpolished treatment. Indeed, he remarks that Rembrandt's youthful works were executed with greater patience than the rest. And he adds that, in the last few years of his life, Rembrandt worked so quickly that, seen from close up, his paintings appear to have been produced with a mason's trowel. According to him, Rembrandt would ask those who came near his works to step back, saying: 'The smell of the colour would upset you.'

The unfinished appearance of certain pictures was also commented upon by other authors. In Baldinucci's opinion it was a result of slowness rather than speed of execution—if a painting was dry, the artist would go back to work on it 'so that sometimes the colour was thicker than half a finger.'

In his *Entretiens sur les vies et sur les ouvrages des plus excellents peintres anciens et modernes* (1685), André Félibien also wrote that 'often he (Rembrandt) would merely slap the colours on with the brush and pile them up in very thick layers, one next to the other without softening them or toning them down to fit in with each other. However, tastes being different, several people have set a high value on these works. At the same time, it is true that there are many kinds of art and that he produced some very fine heads. Although not all of them are gracefully painted, they are extremely forceful; and when they are viewed from a suitable distance they make an excellent effect and look very harmonious.' To which Félibien's interlocutor Pymandre replies: 'Not long ago I was shown one; the tints were separated and the brushwork was marked by such an extraordinary thickness of colours that, when viewed from fairly close up, there was something frightful about the face.' None the less, Félibien continues to uphold his point of view. In his opinion, Rembrandt 'placed tints and half-tints so adroitly and arranged light and shade so felicitously that what he painted roughly, and what often indeed seems to be no more than sketched out, is nevertheless a success providing, as I have said, one does not stand too close.'

Admittedly, these are surprising words to come from the mouth of a theoretician of the Royal Academy of Painting and Sculpture, where normally it was other gods who were venerated and other conceptions which were extolled. Yet in 1721 another member of the same academy, its director Antoine Coypel, made this fine comprehensive statement: 'Those works of Rembrandt which seem the most thickly painted and the most rapidly executed are in fact painted with infinite care, and are as smooth and rounded as those of Correggio, in which one does not notice the application of the paint.' One can only conclude from these quotations that Rembrandt was better understood by the members of the French Academy than by Gerard de Lairesse and Arnold Houbraken who in fact referred to the Academy to justify their reservations. Nevertheless, it was still to be a long time before Rembrandt was universally regarded as one of the most profound and brilliant artists who ever lived. Even when, in 1851, Eugéne Delacroix wrote in his *Journal:* 'Rembrandt may yet be considered a far greater painter than Raphael', he thought it necessary to add: 'I write this blasphemy, which is calculated to make the hair of all the academics stand on end, without taking sides in any way . . .'

Nowadays no one would dream of regarding this as a blasphemous statement. Not that we do not feel close to Raphael—his name could be replaced by others. For if there are certainly old masters whose art is more exotic than Rembrandt's, more harmonious, refined, or pure, there are few who get across to us so directly and so profoundly.

Whether one visits a collection where he is well-represented or reads a book in which his masterworks are reproduced alongside those of his rivals, he always commands attention. And his work is compelling not only for its artistic originality, but also for its human qualities of intensity and warmth. Rembrandt was not merely concerned with painting but also with life and its meaning for mankind, which can endure so much without complaint.

If one finds a gallery where work from his mature period, when he was asserting the whole of his authority, hangs side by side with works by his compatriots, and compares them, Rembrandt's is like that of nobody else (which does not mean that others, having come under his influence, cannot resemble him). Obviously, the prime difference is one of stature, but he also differs by the nonconformist individualism of his character. After the period of roughly ten years when he was the most fashionable portraitist in Amsterdam, he always swam against the tide. In many instances, the very subjects of his works are not ones that one normally associates with 17th century Dutch painting. And while all around him polished technique and painstaking draughtsmanship were triumphant, Rembrandt adopted a style which grew more and more bold, replacing concern for precision with intensity of expression.

Some of his detractors have criticised his taste for ugliness and coarseness. In fact, with the exception of a few of his early works, he can be said to have behaved like a visionary in a society with a fondness for realism. But he does not rank among those who substituted pretty, idealized images for harsh truth. He transformed reality by imbuing it with spirituality: he portrayed subjects without descending to mere anecdote; he told stories, but did not seek to entertain; he conveyed feelings gravely and lyrically, but never lapsed into sentimentality.

There are some very remarkable painters who are not always appreciated except by a small number of connoisseurs. There are others who arouse the enthusiasm of the masses together with that of the most demanding cognoscenti. Those in the first category are preoccupied by problems of technique; they are believers in a painting which is—more or less—pure; they wish the meaning of their works to lie above all in the forms they contain. The artists in the second category, while certainly not unaware of the importance of the pictorial factor, are very much concerned with expression—the expression which can be read on a face or in an attitude, or which results from an action.

However, the very thing which explains the favour they enjoy is often also the cause of a misunderstanding, for many people are tempted to see only expression in their works and remain blind to purely artistic creation. But for Rembrandt as much as for any other great painter, this creation was in no way a secondary consideration. Of course, it would be wrong to neglect the importance of subject-matter in his work, but it would be equally wrong to let oneself be hypnotized by it. Similarly, it would be wrong to ignore his narrative and theatrical aspects, but it would be just as wrong to fail to recognise the artist, the man of colour, light, paint, and, in his etchings and drawings, patch and line. It must not be forgotten that Rembrandt himself tended, towards the end of his life, to reduce narrative elements in favour of more eloquent use of materials.

Does this mean that there are affinities between his art and that of the 20th century? If he was dear to Expressionists like Rouault, Soutine, Nolde and Permeke, neither the Fauves nor the Cubists, still less the Surrealists, can have regarded him as a guiding light. They differed from him in both technique and subject-matter, and his moral atmosphere was no less alien to them than his palette and his chiaroscuro. If the main creators of modern art had been asked to name the old painters who most helped them to discover their style, Rembrandt would rarely have figured among them.

Yet in 1933, his face cropped up curiously in an etching by Picasso—an indication that he has had a greater influence on some minds than might have been believed. For this appearance was completely unsolicited. 'I had an etching plate,' confides Picasso, 'which had had an accident. I said to myself: it's damaged, so I'll draw any old thing on it. I started to scribble. It became Rembrandt ... I even did another one later with his turban, his furs and his eye, his elephant's eye ...'

That Picasso should have thought of the Dutch master when executing an etching is not strange, for nowhere is Rembrandt more familiar to modern eyes than in his prints and drawings. It is in them that he reached the limits of his boldness, the highest pitch of his expression: as we have noted, the fourth state of *The Three Crosses* is in close proximity to modern abstract art, it is understandable to find non-figurative painters today who feel a special admiration for the creator of such a work. But his pictures, particularly those which he painted towards the end his life, are also closer to us than one might first be inclined to think. All things considered, Rembrandt displayed in his figuration an independence which few Old Masters achieved, even assuming they sought it. He was not only one of the most profound artists, and one of the richest in human qualities, but also, of all the masters of the past, one of the freest and boldest.

Ill. 107

List of Illustrations

Page numbers in italics indicate colour plates

269

Bibliography

Eugène Fromentin – *Les Maîtres d'autrefois,* Paris 1875;
C. Hofstede de Groot – *Die Urkunden über Rembrandt,*
The Hague 1906;
Wilhelm R. Valentiner – *Rembrandt, Des Meisters Gemälde,*
Stuttgart 1908;
A.-C. Coppier – *Les Eaux-fortes authentiques de Rembrandt,*
Paris 1929;
A. Bredius, *Rembrandt, Sämtliche Gemälde,* Vienna 1935;
W. Cuendet – *Rembrandt/Radierungen,* Zürich 1947;
Roger Avermaete – *Rembrandt et son temps,* Paris 1952;
Seymour Slive – *Rembrandt and his critics (1630–1730),*
The Hague 1953; Catalogue of the 1956 exhibition of paintings and
drawings at the Rijksmuseum, Amsterdam;
Otto Benesch – *Rembrandt,* Geneva 1957;
Paul Zumthor – *La vie quotidienne en Hollande au temps de
Rembrandt,* Paris 1959;
Kurt Bauch – *Rembrandt, Gemälde,* Berlin 1966;
Kenneth Clark – *Rembrandt and the Italian Renaissance,*
London 1966.

Index